AF710587

Contents

WOMEN RAINMAKERS' 101+ BEST MARKETING TIPS

Theda C. Snyder, Editor

AMERICAN BAR ASSOCIATION ABA SECTION OF LAW PRACTICE MANAGEMENT

Cover and interior design by Catherine Zaccarine.

The Section of Law Practice Management, American Bar Association, offers an educational program for lawyers in practice. Books and other materials are published in furtherance of that program. Authors and editors of publications may express their own legal interpretations and opinions, which are not necessarily those of either the American Bar Association or the Section of Law Practice Management unless adopted pursuant to the By-laws of the Association. The opinions expressed do not reflect in any way a position of the Section or the American Bar Association.

© 1994 American Bar Association. All rights reserved.
Printed in the United States of America.

Library of Congress Catalog Card Number 94-071006
ISBN 0-89707-982-5

95 96 97 98 5 4 3 2

Discounts are available for books ordered in bulk. Special consideration is given to state bars, CLE programs, and other bar-related organizations. Inquire at Publications Planning and Marketing, American Bar Association, 750 N. Lake Shore Drive, Chicago, Illinois 60611.

Foreword

This is the book you've been waiting for—a simple, succinct collection of rainmaking tips that work. For several years, the Women Rainmakers Interest Group has conducted programs, promoted networking, and produced materials on that most practical of lawyering skills: getting clients. It is no secret that many successful lawyers have built a strong client base through effective personal marketing, competent service, and meaningful communication. Nor is it news to state that the lawyers who have the clients often hold a disproportionate amount of influence in their firms.

The Women Rainmakers have attracted a wide variety of practitioners from different sized firms and different geographic locations, all of whom recognized the importance of rainmaking skills. WRIG programs have attracted more than a few men who observed that these women were dealing with the subject of rainmaking in a very creative way.

Women Rainmakers' 101+ Best Marketing Tips is a follow-up to *Women Rainmakers: The Last Frontier,* a collection of speeches by some of the most successful women rainmakers in the country. *101+ Best Marketing Tips* started with the collected suggestions from attendees at WRIG programs. These amorphous pearls were then organized, edited, and in some cases expanded by Theda Snyder, one of the first cochairs of the Women Rainmakers. Her efforts have resulted in a product that captures the dynamism, synergy, and practicality of the live programs in a format that can be digested quickly and easily.

The LPM Publishing Board, several of whom are also active in WRIG, believes that *101+ Best Marketing Tips* will prove to be as valuable and widely read as its predecessor. Any reader interested in the Women Rainmaker Interest Group or marketing generally should contact the American Bar Association Section of Law Practice Management, at 750 North Lake Shore Drive, Chicago, IL 60611.

Professor Gary A. Munneke
Chair, LPM Publishing

Introduction

At the 1990 American Bar Association Annual Meeting in Chicago, the Section of Law Practice Management was the primary sponsor of a program entitled "The Last Frontier: Women Lawyers as Rainmakers and Litigators." As a result of the tremendous response to that program, Martha Africa led the push to establish the Women Rainmakers Interest Group and served as one of its first cochairs. This group has met semiannually and published *Leadership and Management Directions,* the quarterly newsletter of the Management Division interest groups. This book collects the best of that information.

All of the tips in this book were provided by real women rainmakers—including the editor—and their friends. Many tips are presented here in quotation marks to show they are in the lawyer's own voice.

Thanks to the following women rainmakers and supporters of women rainmakers and others whose names may not have been recorded who suggested marketing tips for inclusion in this book:

Nelea Absher, Martha Fay Africa, Lynn Allinghan, Edna R. S. Alvarez, Susan Andrews, Jean Barnum, Suzanne Bass, Kathleen A. Berry, Veronica Boda, Donna Bowling, Vickie Brandt, Mary Bryant, Michelle Cain, Chuck Coulter, Donna Cowan, Karen Crawford, Joe Davis, Suzanne Duvall, Dale Ellis, Elaine Epstein, Terry Feddel, Terence Fenelon, Tresi Freemyer, Sharla Frost, Susan Gaddy, Helaine Gregory, Judith Grubner, Judge Linda Hack, Mary C. Harlan, Gretchen Harris, Ann Houle, Irene Jackson, Miriam Jacobson, Beth Johnson, Joan Kennedy, Donna Killoughey,

Chandlee Kuhn, Julie Landau, Dixie Laswell, Gail Lopes, Karen Mathis, Michelle Mendez, Retta Miller, F. Beth Morgan, Susan Nycum, Ralph Perry, Linda Ravdin, Leslie Regenstein, Gerald A. Riskin, Ruth Rodriguez, Ann Saegert, Carol Schlein, Linda Schoonmaker, Martha Schoonover, Laura Sharp, Sid Shinberg, Gilda Turitz, Ann McNaughton Turner, Cindy Rhodes Victor, Louise Videau, Michael Wald, Ellen S. Wayne, Patricia Wendall.

This book is presented on the RAM principle: Some suggestions may not be appropriate for you, and these you will *reject.* Others will fit your personal style, and these you will *accept.* Another group will not be exactly right, but the tips will work once you *modify* them.

Not every tip is appropriate for every lawyer. Indeed, some tips are contradictory. Each tip worked for the person who suggested it. By selectively using the RAM principle, you will find the ones that create rain for your law practice.

Theda C. Snyder
Encino, California

Chapter 1

Your Marketing Plan

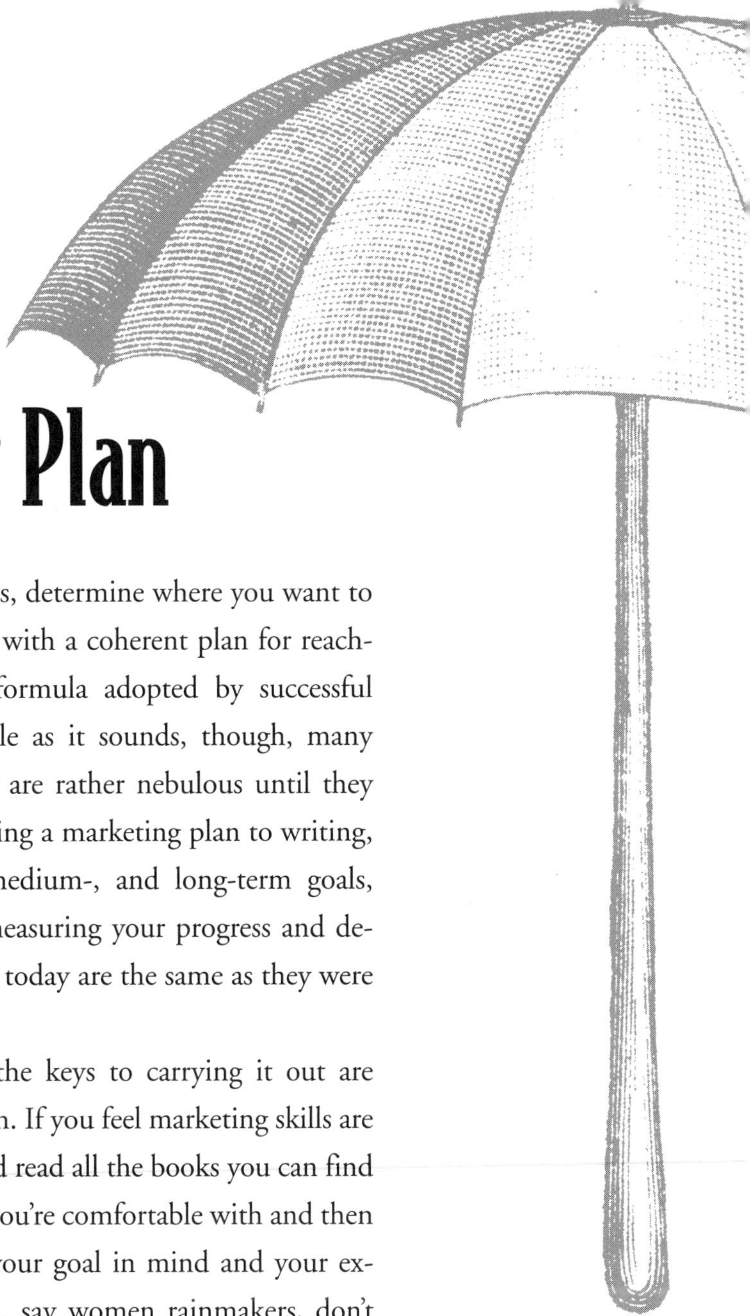

Know what your market is, determine where you want to fit into it, and then come up with a coherent plan for reaching your goals. That's the formula adopted by successful women rainmakers. As simple as it sounds, though, many lawyers find their aspirations are rather nebulous until they put them on paper. Committing a marketing plan to writing, and differentiating short-, medium-, and long-term goals, gives you a benchmark for measuring your progress and determining whether your goals today are the same as they were a year ago or five years ago.

Once you have a plan, the keys to carrying it out are preparation and determination. If you feel marketing skills are lacking, take a few courses and read all the books you can find on the subject. Choose tools you're comfortable with and then use them—every day. Keep your goal in mind and your expectations realistic. Above all, say women rainmakers, don't give up.

Conduct a self-assessment:

Where are you now? Where do you want to be? How are you going to get there? Consider short-, medium-, and long-term goals.

1. Know where you're going—and not just in your career. Where are you going with your life, and where do you want to end up? Imagine that you're at your own funeral! Your friends and family, your professional colleagues, and the people from your church or some civic organization in which you're a member are going to talk about you and what they remember of you. Imagine what you want to hear them say. Then work backward to where you want to go with your life from here. How do your professional circumstances and professional goals fit with your life goals? You must be comfortable with yourself, in touch with who you are and where you want to go, before mechanical marketing tips about developing client relations, maintaining client relations, utilizing and building networks will work for you.

Recent surveys show a high degree of dissatisfaction among lawyers, especially among women lawyers. Being a rainmaker is not a guarantee of job satisfaction, but the benefits and prestige that result from controlling your own business go a long way toward assuring personal career fulfillment.

2. "You have to know your niche. For years there were clients who adored my work but would not send me cases. I had good rapport with our principal client's local office personnel. But the home office staff (all men) did not understand that when they had a 'bet the company' case, I was the one to handle it. Rather, they would send these cases to the senior partner, who in turn assigned it to me.

"I felt frustrated until I stopped to consider. My firm had had good relations with the client. We were getting all the business they could send us. For me to compete with one of the men in my firm wasn't a good use of my time. I went back and reevaluated where I was getting my cases from and if I was shaking every bit of business out of those areas. When I did that, doors opened up, my life got much better, and things got much easier.

"Know who you are and where your business comes from. Also, recognize there are some walls you just don't need to be running into. It is a matter of carefully evaluating who you are and who your clientele is. Most important, learn that while building and maintaining a client base is never easy, you should never, never give up."

Make your marketing goals realistic.

An unattainable goal will discourage you from setting goals at all. Overachieving, even if only you know about it, is much more satisfying.

Maintain a global viewpoint. What trends may affect your practice? At one time antitrust lawyers were very busy. Later, some highly respected antitrust firms folded, with disastrous economic results for some partners. Fifteen years ago concentrating in environmental law was unheard of. Keep an eye out for events and concerns that could impact your practice's viability or present new opportunities.

Sometimes you can segue into a lucrative practice by starting on the other side. For example, if you want to work in employment law, it may be easier to learn the area doing plaintiff's work with the help of an experienced cocounsel. With sufficient experience and expertise, you can market yourself on the management side.

3. "Take courses on marketing. I have taken courses on public relations sponsored by a weekly business magazine and a sales course given by a company that does mostly in-house courses for national sales staffs. I learned the nuts and bolts of how to prepare and issue press releases in the former. I learned important sales techniques to use in talking to clients in the latter. These included establishing preliminary rapport, overcoming objections, and handling complaints. In both places I met new

Focus on what needs to be done.

Don't go off in 20 directions at once.

people, handed out cards, and made valuable business contacts."

Three ingredients for successful marketing:

- Bar association activities
- Lecturing
- Competent and caring client service

4. Prepare a written marketing plan. Studies show that entrepreneurs who have a written business plan do better financially than those without such a plan. It can be as simple as handwritten notes on a legal pad.

Define your target market and the tools you will use to reach that market. Set verifiable and specific goals: e.g., "one new case a month from increased visibility in the north suburban market by writing a family law column in the neighborhood newspaper." Include specific actions that must be taken to achieve the goal and time lines for reaching the objectives. Review and revise your plan frequently. Analyze and change what doesn't work.

The most important part of the marketing plan is a section outlining objectively verifiable goals. Examples are "two new lender liability cases in the coming year" or "increase gross revenues 15 percent for the year." The more specific your goal, the better. "Improve client relations" is not an objectively verifiable goal. "Develop a client questionnaire and distribute by May 1" is.

5. The degree of formality appropriate for your plan depends largely on how many people will rely on it. If you're the only one who will use the plan, handwritten notes in a loose-leaf notebook will do. Devote separate pages to short-, medium-, and long-term goals. Keep a log of your marketing activities. Diary a specific date to compare your progress to your goals.

If you are using your marketing plan as part of your presentation to a lender, naturally you will want to present it as attractively as possible.

The plan of a plaintiff's personal injury attorney who wants to start or increase her medical malpractice caseload might look like this:

Means

- Publish an article in the local bar journal in the next 12 months on new trends in medical malpractice litigation.
- Go out to lunch with another lawyer who may be a referral source once a week.
- Join the medical malpractice subcommittee of the bar association within 30 days; attend at least 75 percent of the meetings over the next 12 months.
- Report all favorable medical malpractice case dispositions to the appropriate news medium within 48 hours.

Ends

- Bring in five new medical malpractice cases within the next six months.
- Increase number of new medical malpractice cases to two per month for months 6–12.

After you reach the goal of two new malpractice cases a month, increase the target to three or four a month for the next 12-month period.

Here is the plan of an attorney seeking tort defense business. The target market niche has been defined as insurance carriers, risk management companies, and major self-insureds. This rainmaker has collected information from industry journals and the state department of insurance to create a list of prospective

In developing your marketing plan,

think small at the beginning; don't bite off more than you can chew.

It is not going to happen overnight.

The plan you put into effect today will take a long time to come to fruition. Some things may happen quickly; others may require years to result in a client. Start tomorrow.

clients, which she keeps in the inside pocket of the notebook. The notebook also contains an activity log, where the attorney notes all her ideas and activities by date. Her goals are:

Short-Term Goals (Six Months)

- Make one new contact per week.
- Follow up by telephone on contacts made in recent trip to St. Louis.
- Attend one bar association meeting per month.
- Develop media outlet list for press releases and send out at least one release.

Medium-Term Goals (One Year)

- Have personal caseload of at least ten cases from at least one carrier.
- Visit current risk management company client in Atlanta.
- Visit major airline prospect in New York City.

Long-Term Goals (Five Years)

- Partnership

6. Don't give up. Marketing is an exceedingly slow process. You can make a successful presentation to 200 people—everyone is clapping and the evaluations are terrific. You're sure the phone will be ringing off the hook Monday morning, but nothing happens. On the other hand, you might have people calling you who say they took your course 15 years ago, and they kept the handout.

A widespread theory says it takes six contacts to make a sale. Keep contacting that potential client. Keep publicizing your practice. When clients need a lawyer, they often contact the one they heard about most recently. Make sure it's you.

7. One theory is that a lawyer should spend 20 percent of her time marketing. It's a difficult goal, especially when you are in the crunch of what you are doing, but you have to commit to the effort. Keep your ultimate goal in mind: achieving the independence that results from managing your own client base.

A rainmaker never has idle time, no matter how new or slow her practice.

Devote every available spare minute to marketing. This could be as simple as lining up a lunch date or writing a law review article about a new Supreme Court decision.

Complete one marketing task every day.

How often does a rainmaker market? The answer is *every day.* This isn't as onerous as you might think. The best marketing techniques are simple daily tasks, such as reading and forwarding articles of interest to clients. It's getting out of the office. It's planning.

At first, setting aside time on a daily basis may seem impossible in your busy world. However, with practice, marketing will become habitual.

Browse the business section of your local bookstore. You will find plenty of marketing books. Sometimes it's important to learn the marketing perspective of nonlawyers. You can adapt and shape the suggestions for your law practice.

8. Follow-through is one of the most difficult marketing tasks. For example, let's say you were fortunate enough to obtain an invitation to deliver a major speech. Follow through by asking the sponsor to send you some extra brochures to send to your clients and referral sources. Your effort is only half effective if you spent 200 hours preparing and writing extensive course materials but do not take the time to send out the brochures. Or, after the seminar, rework the course materials into a short item for the local legal newspaper, where other lawyers who may

Create a marketing budget.

Review your financial records and commit to spending a percentage of last year's revenue on marketing. Decide on what marketing tools the money will be spent—advertising, brochure design and printing, etc.

become referral sources could read it. Allocate time and effort to achieve the biggest impact from every marketing outreach.

Survey clients and others about their reaction to your efforts.

9. Choose marketing tools you are comfortable with. Teach if you enjoy it. Don't try it if you don't. The same holds true for writing articles, television ads, or any marketing tool you can think of.

In a small firm, partners can assign each other marketing tasks; e.g., contact three former clients we have lost touch with.

Not every marketing outreach will be successful; some may be dismal failures.

Direct mail is not as easy as it looks. One rainmaker reports sending 7,500 pieces to small businesses with no response other than two calls from other lawyers looking for work.

Think twice before joining a collective television advertising program. The expense is huge, and a lot of the cases are tiny or not meritorious. Not only will you spend a lot of money, but your commitment to the service includes taking the "loss leader" calls too. The combination can be deleterious to your mental health as well as your pocketbook.

10. Assess your strengths and your position in the market. For example, if you decide you want to develop a practice in a specific area, you'll need to answer these questions:

- Do you have the skills necessary to do the work successfully?
- Are there other fields that might be more profitable or desirable?
- Do you have a base of practice on which to build?

- Do you have contacts that might help you build a practice base in that area?
- Does this practice area offer relatively easy entry, or is it saturated?

"I still track all new clients. I put new information in their file, on their Rolodex card, on their client card, and in my left-hand drawer. You may think most of your business comes from a certain source. With tracking, you may be surprised to learn that when you look at dollar amounts, it comes from another."

Many lawyers, especially those new in practice, are reluctant to send any potential client away. That's a mistake. Take only the clients who fit your profile. Send all the others to other lawyers and let them know what kind of clients you're looking for. The referrals you get back will more than compensate for those you sent.

Integrate the personal and business parts of your life to achieve your goals in both.

Rather than have marketing monopolize your valuable time, learn to socialize while at a trade association or develop business while at a birthday party.

11. Keep a log of your marketing activities. Diary a specific date to compare your progress to your goals.

Here is a sample log page for an attorney seeking corporate work who sets aside one morning a week for marketing:

2/17/92

Prospects

1. ABC Products Corp.
   123 Main St.
   Aliso Viejo, CA 92656 062/555–9876
   Contact former client Tom Brown.

No longer with company, now with Big & Huge in San Francisco; new CFO says send him firm brochure. [Follow-up date diaried]

Diary dates to review how well you have met your plan's goals, just as you would diary case review.

You won't always have met your goals. However, each new review will energize you to redouble your efforts.

2. Honeybee Laboratories
   Industrial Park
   Metropolis, Georgia 34567
   123/555–4321. Referred by Betty Lou. Spoke with John Smith, says does all foreseeable legal work in house.

To do

- Thank you note to Mike Morris for Herman referral
- Make lunch date with Bob Carson.

12. A lot of marketing is attitude. If you think you can't attract business, you won't.

The secret of success is following the lessons of *The Little Engine That Could.*

Visualize success.

Chapter 2

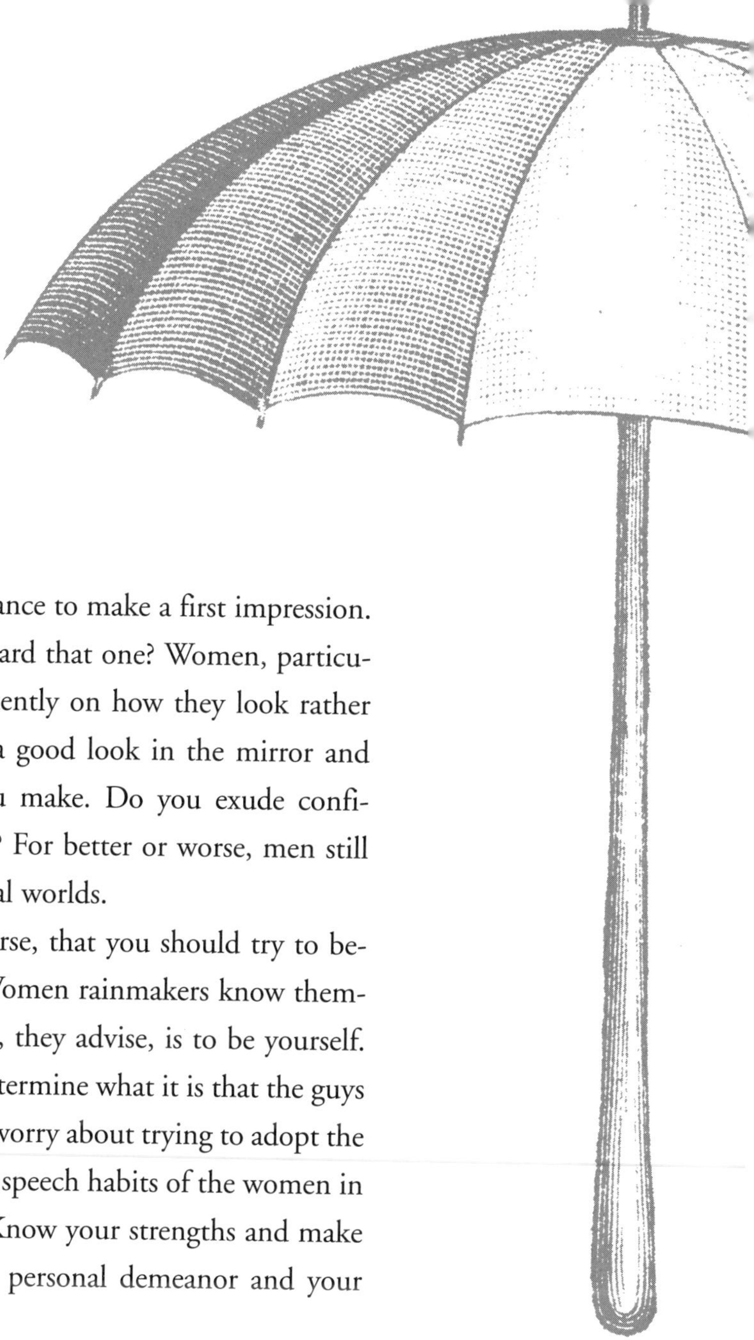

Image

You never get a second chance to make a first impression. How many times have you heard that one? Women, particularly, seem to be judged frequently on how they look rather than on what they do. Take a good look in the mirror and consider what impression you make. Do you exude confidence, knowledge, and power? For better or worse, men still dominate the business and legal worlds.

That doesn't mean, of course, that you should try to become something you're not. Women rainmakers know themselves well. The key to success, they advise, is to be yourself. Don't worry about trying to determine what it is that the guys do that works for them. Don't worry about trying to adopt the dress or the mannerisms or the speech habits of the women in the office who made partner. Know your strengths and make sure they're projected by your personal demeanor and your professional trappings.

A career woman has to look like a lady, act like a man, and work like a dog.

13. "Your first step must be to analyze yourself. Who are you? What do you feel comfortable doing? It makes no sense to wear somebody else's clothes if they don't fit you. On the other hand, my experience tells me that sometimes you have capabilities that you're unaware of. I had no clients for five years while in a prior firm. Now I have a well-established practice. I didn't change. I was the same person, but my sense of myself and what I needed to do changed. I think anyone can start from zero and create a practice if you're competent, imaginative, and enthusiastic and you put your energy into it."

Consider your personal image. What is your personal image? As a rainmaker you are on display, as it were, virtually 24 hours a day. You're not going to do something that you don't want somebody to gossip about later. Does that mean you have to walk around in a gray flannel suit and a white shirt and one of those cute little bow ties we were all wearing a few years ago? No, it doesn't. Making a strong personal statement, whether you wear a hat or an interesting piece of jewelry, is fine. But consider as you are out and about on your daily activities—and not just from Monday through Friday—what personal image statement you make. That isn't only a visual statement. Every person you meet is a potential client; keep that in mind in considering the personal image that you convey to the people you meet seven days a week, 24 hours a day.

14. Internal marketing within your firm is as important as—or more important than—outside marketing. Others must feel confident about bringing you in on a matter. Assess how you are perceived. Evaluate positioning yourself, staying away from killer partners, affiliating with a mentor.

"I spent years trying to be a conservative male, and obviously for a woman it was an impossible task. Having been in private practice now for three or four years, I find that the friends that I developed inside client companies are the people that I really let get to know me, rather than the people for whom I put on a face trying to resemble the people I saw being successful. They became wonderful clients."

15. View your gender as an advantage that helps you stand out from the crowd. Don't try to be a man clone.

Deciding whether or not to emphasize your gender is an important threshold issue. Some women lawyers specifically market themselves as women. Typically these are family lawyers. However, many women—though not overtly—remind clients of the advantages of their gender. These might include putting the other side off guard or just being a good listener.

16. Develop the image that you are a good rainmaker, and you will be perceived as one.

17. Despite all the books and articles on the subject, some women still don't understand how important it is to look businesslike. Big hair is out. So are microskirts and cleavage-revealing necklines. If you look like a "babe," you won't get respect, let alone business.

Some men can adopt far-out fashions with success: ponytails, cowboy regalia in northern climes, and feminine-looking fur coats. Regrettably, though, women are still best advised to adopt a conservative look. Since a good rainmaker attracts business everywhere she goes, plan on keeping the conservative persona 24 hours a day for a long, long time.

The illusion of success is important.

In answer to "How's it going?" say "Business is fabulous" rather than "Things are slow." Fake it till you make it. Stop being so modest!

Clients care that their lawyers tried, regardless of whether the case was won or lost.

Let the client see all the effort you expend on his or her behalf. Send the client copies of everything you receive or produce.

Do you have a personal trademark? One successful woman rainmaker with a bankruptcy practice wears a gold and diamond scale of justice brooch every day. Another well-known woman wears a hat every day. Trademarks make you memorable. They set you apart from the crowd and work as conversation pieces.

18. As a solo, you can afford to do only certain work, and you don't want to attract the whole universe. Being a solo carries the implication that you're going to be doing the work; the client will be dealing with you and not with a huge entity. That is a selling point.

19. Your business card is the one item you probably give to everyone. What does it say about you? Consider paper grade and color and print style. Make sure the print is large enough to read easily.

What about a dignified logo for use on your stationery, business cards, checks, and advertising? A scale of justice logo is pretty standard and can be ordered through just about any printer. A computer graphics consultant can inexpensively design a custom logo.

20. Take a look at your office. Is your reception room attractive? Are the periodicals appropriate? Art with legal themes, bar association informational brochures, and laudatory plaques and certificates all reassure the current and potential clients in your office.

Put informational brochures in your waiting room. Many bar associations publish these for bulk purchase. Usually they deal with consumer and personal law issues such as buying a home or what to do if arrested. Some pamphlets also address small business issues. Two excellent examples are the newsletter *Client Update* and the brochure *Your Law.* Further information and free samples are available from the ABA Service Center, 312/988–5522. You can also purchase similar items through Excelsior Legal Supply, 800/221–2972.

Keep copies of articles and columns you've had published in a notebook in the reception area. Clients are usually impressed and sometimes will retain you for work in an area they hadn't realized you handle.

21. Use technology as a marketing tool. Let clients know that your computer systems are state-of-the-art, that you spend the money to stay on the leading edge to better serve your clientele. Then make sure you do indeed utilize your equipment to its full potential.

22. Have a sense of humor.

Check your state's ethical rulings on use of a trade name that describes what you do.

One lawyer has had great success promoting her practice as the Women's Law Center.

Chapter 3

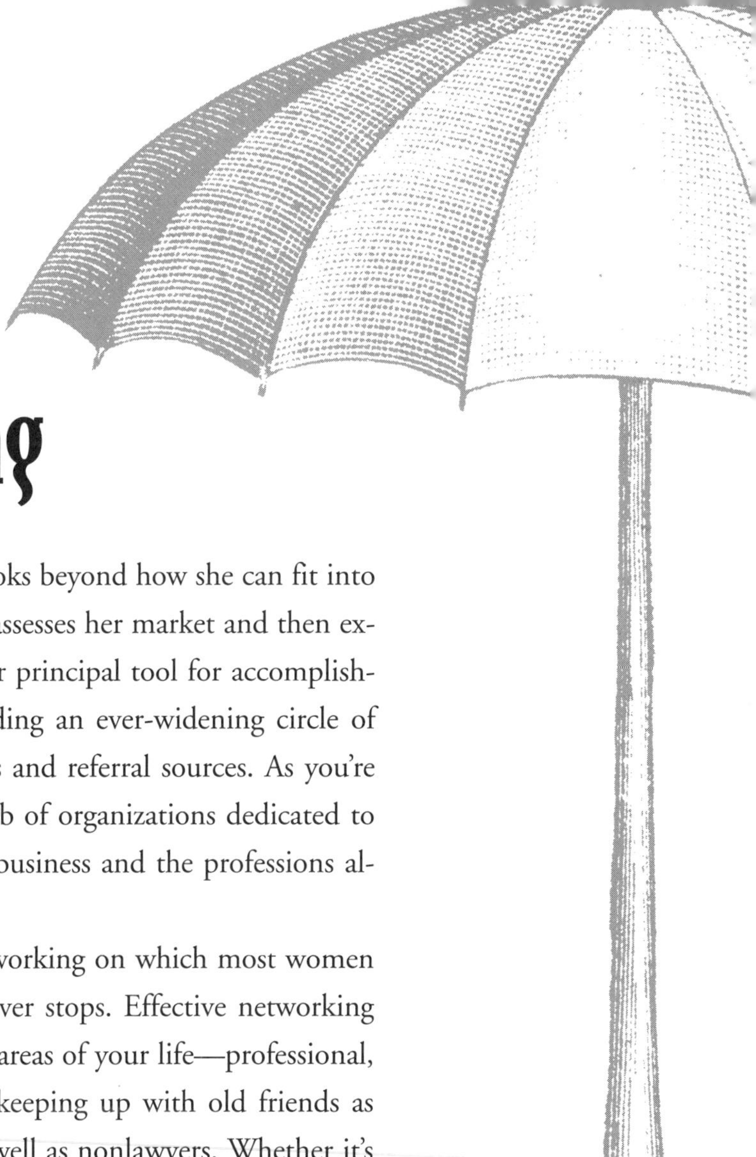

Networking

A successful rainmaker looks beyond how she can fit into an existing marketplace. She assesses her market and then expands it to suit her goals. Her principal tool for accomplishing this is networking—building an ever-widening circle of contacts as prospective clients and referral sources. As you're undoubtedly aware, a vast web of organizations dedicated to the promotion of women in business and the professions already exists.

The one point about networking on which most women rainmakers agree is that it never stops. Effective networking means making contacts in all areas of your life—professional, civic, social, academic—and keeping up with old friends as well as new, other lawyers as well as nonlawyers. Whether it's a bar activity or a charity event, your participation gives you valuable exposure that may pay off when you least expect it.

Treat each person with whom you come in contact as a potential client.

23. You've been networking all your life. Networking is simply building a circle of contacts. The more people you know, the more likely you are to get business from among those contacts.

24. Young lawyers should get involved in *anything:* politics, church, health club. Get out of the office.

Start making your contacts and building your personal relationships with business and professional people while you are still in school. Join one to three targeted groups as a student member and become active in the group.

25. Besides knowing how to network, you have to figure out where to do it. Answer: be a joiner.

Which Organization?

The first question is what to join. Here are some options:

- Bar associations—your best referrals come from other lawyers
- Women's business groups—mixed or single industry (e.g., Women in Real Estate)
- Philanthropic—charity boards
- Religious or ethnic—don't forget your church or synagogue
- Traditional "old boy" networks; e.g., Rotary Club

Joining alone isn't enough. Active participation through regular attendance at meetings and committee leadership distinguishes you as a go-getter. Of course, if you take on a task, you must complete it competently. The idea is to give people a chance to get to know you for the bright, capable person you are.

Be Choosy

Join selectively. Choose an organization in which you have a genuine interest. Others will bore you. Besides, it's hard to work up enthusiasm for a goal you don't really care about.

More is not necessarily better. If you spread yourself too thin, you can't make a meaningful contribution anywhere. You'll just be a name on a mailing list. That doesn't benefit you as a rainmaker at all.

Don't overlook the networks you already have.

Your friends, neighbors, former classmates from every level represent important networking resources.

Appropriate Expectations

Give any organization a fair chance. After all, there was something about it that originally attracted you. But if you discover the membership isn't right for you demographically, or you're just not enjoying it, quit and move on. There are so many organizations out there these days, you're sure to find another that better meets your needs.

Don't be pushy with other members. Soft sell always works best. Let people know what you do, but appreciate people for their diversity, their friendship. If you value people only as prospective clients, your mercenary attitude will quickly be obvious and turn them off. On the other hand, let people know (within ethical bounds) that you do want them as clients and their referrals. Some people think if you project a successful image you don't need any more clients!

Don't expect results right away. A year after starting active participation is not too long to wait. In the meantime, enjoy the organization's activities. You may be surprised at the personal satisfaction you derive.

26. Networking is building a circle of contacts. As a dedicated marketer, devote yourself to expanding your contacts. Join and become active in several organizations. Pick a group that you will enjoy. It might be a fraternal order, a charity board, a political volunteer group, or an industry trade association. Just showing up and dealing out your cards is not

Keep up your contacts with your college and law school classmates.

enough to gain people's confidence. Count on attending regular meetings and participate in committee work. Organizational work offers a showcase to highlight how well organized, thorough, and capable you are. The more people you know, the more likely you are to get business from among those contacts.

Think of the people that you come in contact with at church and in the activities that you do just for fun as possible clients or as possible referrals. Even if that person's professional activities are completely irrelevant to yours, let him or her know what you do. If that person is your friend, he or she will likely refer another friend or family member in need of your particular skills.

27. "Get active in one or more bar associations. I have found that the best referrals come from other lawyers. Your bar association can promote you. Bar associations love workers. You have to get active. Your bar association can give you legitimacy. The association can give you visibility. I'm very nice to the association staff. The staff like me, so the editor of the bar newspaper did a feature on me. The purpose of the article was to promote the association activities in which I was involved, but it also heightened my personal visibility in the legal community in a very favorable way. Your bar association can help you. Don't take those staff people for granted; do not treat them with other than respect and courtesy and affection, because they can help you a lot."

"I can't overemphasize getting involved in bar activities. One of the things I have done is take other lawyers who are in litigation sections in larger firms to lunch and dinner or whatever and tell them—you have to open your mouth and say 'I want your business.' Tell these lawyers that when they have conflicts in this area, that's what you want. You are not trying to compete with them or take their clients away from them. Let them know you are there, and of course your reputation must precede you. They need to know you are available to take those conflict situations."

If the organization you chose to join generates no business over a year and bores you to tears besides, it's time to move on.

Join the ABA Section of Law Practice Management and the Women Rainmakers Interest Group. You automatically receive a subscription to *Law Practice Management* magazine, which is chock-full of all kinds of helpful information. Every issue has at least one article with a practical marketing tip.

28. "I try to belong to national organizations within my specialty. In estate administration there's lots of cross-jurisdictional work, and I have gotten probably my best referrals that way. One of the greatest sources has been the American College of Trust and Estate Counselors."

There are lots of reasons to consider joining a specialized national bar association. It's a great way to brainstorm with practitioners in your field. Your local competitors may not want to share their hottest tips, but someone from another state is likely to be more forthcoming. The group's publications will be particularly helpful. Additionally, there is the prospect of referrals.

Here are some national groups you might consider:

- Commercial Law League of America (Collection and bankruptcy), 312/781–2000
- National Association of Social Security Claimants' Representatives, 201/444–1415
- American Immigration Lawyers Association, 202/371–9377
- National Employment Lawyers Association, 415/227–4655
- American Academy of Adoption Attorneys, 602/262–5841 (1994–95 president's office)

"What has worked best for me in developing client relations

is to stay in touch with people who are in organizations that either are clients or are likely clients. They become my friends, and I nurture those friendships."

- American College of Trust and Estate Counsel, 310/398–1888

The *Encyclopedia of Associations* (available in the public library) lists numerous others.

29. Inclusion in various lists is very helpful. Join trade associations as an affiliate member. That way members know you concentrate in legal issues applicable to that industry and share their point of view. Lawyers from other geographical regions also use the lists to refer business.

It's also helpful to be a member of a law college. The membership list is a great directory to use for referrals.

Don't forget the committee lists for substantive law sections of the American Bar Association. They signal who is expert in a given area.

Rather than a list where anyone can purchase a listing, these lists reflect a lawyer's genuine interest in a specialty evidenced by membership and activity.

In each of these instances, since membership is a prerequisite to list inclusion, of course, the benefits inherent in belonging to the organization are also available: newsletters, writing opportunities, committee activities, conferences and seminars—all excellent ways of generating business.

The U.S. Small Business Administration in cooperation with state governments sponsors Small Business Development Centers. Additionally, there is a separate Office of Women Business Owners within the SBA (contact 202/205–6673). Throughout the nation, either through the SBDCs or directly through OWBO, women's mentoring programs that cross business practice lines are developing. If you want to market to small companies, this is a wonderful way to develop relationships with people who are building businesses.

Emphasize small businesses and help them start up, incorporate, and enter partnership agreements and other business formation and maintenance transactions. As part of your full service to your client, you might offer, "Now that you are doing this, do you have your will up to date? Do you need a new will? How is your estate planned? If it is a fairly simple matter, I can help you, and if it is fairly complex, I can refer you to an estate specialist." This will create business that you can cross-refer within your firm or to an outside colleague.

If you're bad at remembering names,

write down some unique feature about that person on their card so you can later identify him or her.

30. Networking is probably your most important source of marketing leads. Women's organizations can provide new community contacts, opportunities for public speaking, and a forum to exchange ideas with other businesswomen. How many of these organizations are in your city?

- YWCA, the largest women's organization in the United States, has businesswomen's and entrepreneurs' programs
- Business and Professional Women's Clubs (national contact 202/293–1100) has local organizations in every state
- National Network of Women in Sales
- Women in Business, in Management, in Construction, Telecommunications, Film, and in just about every other possible industry you would be interested in courting; these organizations provide a fertile networking ground not dominated by other lawyers

  For partners, shareholders, and solo practitioners only:
- National Association of Women Business Owners (301/608–2590)
- Women Entrepreneurs Network

Go to seminars for businesswomen. Your state may sponsor intensive all-day seminars. Fred Pryor Seminars (800/255–6139)

Many lawyers receive the bulk of their cases from other lawyers' referrals.

Bar association meetings and continuing legal education programs provide excellent opportunities for meeting potential referral sources.

sponsors a broad range of leadership and management seminars designed specifically for women. The Businesswomen's Training Institute (800/423–6540) puts on a program called "The Organized Woman."

Join a businesswomen's group. Many women partners and solos consider National Association of Women Business Owners the best of the bunch. The members are all decision makers. However, you may find a more diversified organization provides a better entree to big business. Besides your local Business and Professional Women's Club, the American Association of University Women and National Organization for Women are possibilities. Even churches and synagogues sponsor businesswomen's groups these days.

There are lots of ways to find local women's organizations. Your newspaper probably publishes a business and/or community events calendar. Look in the yellow pages under "Associations." Look in the white pages under "Women" or "Association." "American" and "National" also yield interesting results. Your mayor's or governor's office may keep a list of women's organizations available to you free of charge. You might be surprised to learn the diversity of organizations in your city or state.

31. Network with attorneys who are both very much senior *and* very much junior to you. Those junior people, especially the ones who are so unsuccessful that they go on to become governors or senators, will remember your kindnesses to them. So be kind to the goofball, low-end new person or marginal lawyer, because the benefit to you can be enormous. At the high end, all you do is ask "How do you do this?" The senior attorneys will be flattered enough that they will spend an hour giving you notes and sending you business.

"Many of us think that the place to get business is from other lawyers who are more experienced and have been around longer. But it's important for lots of reasons, including marketing, to befriend, do favors for, help out, and mentor younger lawyers. I have done that on many occasions, and I have found many of these younger lawyers who have eventually become the same age I am now (some have even surpassed me) have gone on to practice settings where they have business to refer out. They have remembered me and have been grateful for my help and have been a great source of business for me."

Always find a lawyer for clients who are seeking expertise out of your field.

They will continue to call you because you have facilitated their business.

It's a mistake to avoid socializing with low-level employees in a client organization, particularly if you are a junior person yourself. Take your peer to lunch, dinner, the symphony, the theater, the zoo, the botanic garden, or wherever. Just as you are progressing through your career, these people are progressing through their careers. Eventually they will be senior-level engineers or geologists or general counsels and valuable contacts.

32. *Meet and Greet*

Choose an organization you think you would like to be involved with. It might be an industry organization. It might be a women's group. These days, happily, you can combine the two, e.g., Women in Management, Women in Sales, Women in Architecture, Women in Construction, bar associations. One theory holds that one should always put one's name tag on the right shoulder because when one sticks out one's hand to shake hands, it is the part that will go forward.

When you go to networking events, wear something with

If you are a specialist in one legal area, join a women's group or groups that includes many areas of legal specialization.

pockets. Put the cards you are going to give in one pocket and the cards you are going to get in the other. If you go up to somebody and you have to fumble through your purse, by that time the person has walked away. Have your business cards in your pocket and ready. When you get back to your office, write down where you met the person and follow up with a letter.

The hardest part of "meet and greet" is going up to strangers in groups. You feel like an outsider. It is hard. It takes a lot of nerve to go up to people and introduce yourself. Sometimes you find yourself with some other outsider. One technique is, when you find yourself with some other outsider, act like you are an insider: take the other person by the elbow and guide her over to the most important person in the room. Say something like "Paul President, I would like to introduce you to Ann Oakley." Ann thinks you are great, and Paul is trying to remember where he met you before, but it gets you into the group. That is also a way for you to move from cluster to cluster in a group.

The hardest part of cocktail party networking is going up to strangers and introducing yourself. It does get easier with practice! Try to find other loners and form your own group. Practice moving from group to group—don't get stuck with the same people all night. Try to come away from each networking opportunity with ten new business cards.

If you are at all shy about the cocktail reception introduction thing, consider buying *How to Work a Room* by Susan Roane. This book has some very concrete, practical, interesting tips that will help you overcome some of the inherent shyness that more junior lawyers feel about these type of situations.

33. Use software to keep track of information about clients and prospects alike. One such program is Corner Office. For information, call 800/724–2035.

Make friends with your chiropractor and refer patients to him or her.

However, an agreement to swap clientele is an unethical fee-sharing agreement.

Don't delay entering information into your system while you get around to deciding what salutation to use, whether to send a holiday card, or if you should add the name to your newsletter circulation list.

Set up a label system to keep track of contacts that eliminates the guesswork and makes data entry more accurate. Set up a document for a sheet of mailing labels. For example, WordPerfect 5.1/5.2 includes a slick macro called LABELS that automatically sets up the paper size for specific Avery labels.

The "Salutation" abbreviations—first name (FN), nickname (NN), or Mr. or Ms.—are used for correspondence. The company name or last name (LN) is used for an alphabetical sort. The final version of this form lets you quickly circle options.

The LIST field divides the master list into broad groups for mailings: business contacts, vendors, and various bar associations. The NB field can be used to print a smaller version of the database for your Filofax. To avoid lugging around 2,000-plus names, winnow down to the traveling version using this option. As you go through the day, you can note decisions about whether to send a holiday card or newsletter and whether to use the home or office address by circling options on the form. Finally, this form allows you to keep track of where you met people so you can track the success of various outreaches for your business plan. Each label measures 1 by 2⅝ inches, leaving plenty of room on the back to note other comments for eventual data entry.

34. When you give people your business card, put a note on it to remind the recipient of your conversation. They are less likely to throw it away. When they see the card again and see the note, they will think of your conversation.

Send congratulations notes to other lawyers on their accomplishments.

Follow up your networking with a letter or note repeating your pleasure in meeting your new acquaintance. If appropriate, indicate you would be pleased to help that person with the legal issue you discussed briefly. Several business supply houses now sell informal cards printed "Enjoyed meeting you" or "Enjoyed our meeting." You can also find similar greetings at the office supply store. Meticulously avoid outright solicitation of any individual's legal business.

35. Use rotary file cards as your business cards.

36. Don't be stingy about referring business to others. Trying to tackle an area you know nothing about is one of the classic paths to malpractice. Consider who might be right for the client. A client will appreciate receiving two or three names to choose among. You can let all three lawyers know you gave out their names, so they can identify the caller. Even if the client calls none of them, you have created goodwill with those lawyers.

37. Even in very large corporations, if you are working in one area, that may not be the area that is giving out the kind of work you want to do. You have to ask your contact for other names. Once you have a name, you have got an inroad, and you can say "So-and-so referred me to you."

"Our best sources were other lawyers who didn't do bankruptcy work. They would very often send lots and lots of work to us, and the guarantee was we would always send the clients back. We never took their clients."

38. Participate in mentor programs. The U.S. Small Business Administration Office of Women Business Ownership has a program: 202/205–6673. Many women's organizations do too, as does the ABA Section of Law Practice Management: 312/988–5619.

One law school alumni association has a mentoring program that pairs experienced and new attorneys. Experienced lawyers teach rainmaking and other practice management skills. Check if similar programs are available through your alma mater.

39. Refer business to your clients whenever you can. Let them know you were the source.

40. Don't burn your bridges. Stay on good terms with former employers and opposing counsel. They can be significant referral sources.

41. "This is a tip for those of you who came to the law as a second career. I kept up my contacts by writing a letter stating that I am now a lawyer, telling them I now do real estate property work, and asking if they have a building they are buying or selling to please keep me in mind. I have gotten a lot of work that way. If you have had a prior association, even though you are not going to practice in that area, you still have those contacts."

42. Your firm's vendors may be a source of business, either directly or by referral. Manage your vendor relationships as if every vendor were a potential client. Consider multiplying the number of vendors you do business with to increase the likelihood of receiving reciprocal business.

Don't forget your relationship with judges.

Judges have people come to them all the time with their problems, and judges will make referrals.

"If you don't have a niche within your local bar association, create one.

We didn't have a bankruptcy law committee; I was involved in forming one, and now you can guess who is chairman of it."

43. Practice a script for introducing yourself in a networking setting. Strive for action words and be positive. For example, "I help injured people receive fair compensation" is more meaningful than "I'm a personal injury lawyer." Here are some others:

- "I'm a lawyer with Forthright & Honest. We protect your rights in court."
- "I help corporations comply with Delaware's unique corporate laws."
- "I provide cost-effective representation to small businesses like yours."

Create a "cocktail party" description of what you do. This can be as short as a few words but no longer than two sentences. The description should be concrete and stated in terms of what a potential client needs or how a potential client can benefit from your service.

44. What if you've looked around your community, and there is no high-level business women's organization? Start one! Have lunch with those you believe will form the nucleus of your group. Decide how to proceed and divide up the tasks.

If you have a good-size conference room, you can call the organizational meeting in your office. Alternatively, consider getting space in a community building or the banquet room of a restaurant. The problem with the last suggestion is that the restaurant will probably require a deposit, impose a minimum fee, and require attendees to purchase a meal. If you don't get the expected turnout, there could be a financial loss.

Publicize your budding group through the local paper, community access cable television, bulletin board notices, and every other way you can think of. Consider membership requirements: years in business, work in a specific industry, and business ownership are possibilities. Maybe you will welcome any working woman.

Expect to put in some serious time to get the group going. The payoff will be in shared knowledge, networking, and clients.

45. Get active in community affairs as a way to promote yourself and your skills. Every charitable organization needs volunteers and, more importantly, can use your skills and talents on governing boards. Practicing law puts things in perspective and trains you to make well-informed decisions quickly. Charitable and community boards and committees need people with these abilities. Usually other board members are movers and shakers in the community whom you may never otherwise meet. What you do for these groups can be the basis for press releases. The best part is it doesn't feel like marketing.

How you shake hands is often the first impression you leave. How is your handshake?

Dos

- Some men are still reticent to a shake a woman's hand. Extend yours first if necessary.
- Keep your palm perpendicular to the floor.
- Keep four fingers together, thumb up.
- Take the other person's whole hand firmly into your whole hand.
- Shake one to three times—more gets silly.

Don'ts

- Don't curve your fingers down as if you expected your hand to be kissed.

Join the chamber of commerce.

Get out and meet your fellow businesspeople. Shake hands; pass out cards. Offer to speak, work on a committee. Get your name known in the community.

Invite your referral sources for a breakfast.

People are fresh that way.

- Don't loosen your hand as if it were a limp rag.
- Don't grip so hard it seems you're in an arm-wrestling contest.
- Don't use a two-handed handshake except to show affection—rarely in business.

46. Pro bono work can be a marketing tool. If there is a prestige lawyer's organization in your town that does pro bono work, that may be the best networking opportunity. The price of admission is the pro bono case.

You can enter a new practice area through your pro bono work. Nonprofit community organizations are likely to need all kinds of legal services but lack funds for paid counsel. You might offer to represent a citizens' group for a cause you believe in. Your bar association may have a committee that provides legal advice to starving artists. Environmental law, employment discrimination, and intellectual property are three booming fields in which you can get your feet wet through pro bono.

Become a mediator or arbitrator. This gives you access to a whole new group of lawyers. Involvement in alternate dispute resolution is a great way to get to know judges, other lawyers, and potential clients.

47. Go out to lunch. You can't network with a sandwich at your desk. Call up a client, an old classmate, or the new acquaintance you met at a seminar.

Calendar dates to call others to go out for lunch just as you would calendar a reminder date on a case.

"Every month I go to a lunch with a number of (it happens to be women) professionals and attorneys. To keep that from becoming just a friendly monthly lunch, you really have to follow up with the individuals in the meeting. I make it a practice to try, after the lunch, to pick out one of those people I have met to go one-on-one with her. I contact her afterward and say 'It was nice to have lunch with you. Let's get together just you and me.' This way you can build a personal relationship with that person."

Get to know your kids' teachers and parents of their friends.

48. "Take advantage of every opportunity daily life presents. I recently had the opportunity to have lunch with executives of a potential client (an insurance company) where the head person was a woman. The other people at the lunch were men. One of the other people in my firm was very dominating in our conversation at lunch, and I didn't have an opportunity to say very much. Afterward, I happened to be in the ladies' room with this woman and made my points there. Take every opportunity you can. It's the 'new girl connection.'"

49. Personal contacts! Meet as many people as you can.

50. Consider joining a barter association. Barter associations provide a way to turn your excess time into income. Instead of cash, you will receive barter credits. Barter accounts are kept in dollars, and you will bill clients exactly as you would as if they were paying in cash. Of course, you must require any cost advance to be paid in cash since your vendors are unlikely to be in the same barter exchange.

The benefit is you have a built-in market for your services of the other businesses in the exchange who would not likely have come to you otherwise. These members are part of your personal network and are likely to refer cash clients.

The downside is you are limited in your purchases to what

Stay in touch with your alumni association.

Most law schools publish an alumni directory, an invaluable networking tool.

you can buy from the other members. Also, the Internal Revenue Service taxes barter income the same as cash—when you receive it, not when you spend.

One rainmaker who belongs to a barter exchange reports: "I have purchased two phone systems for my office as I grew through the years. I dictate over the phone to my backup barter secretarial service. I purchase everything from office supplies and business Christmas gifts to jewelry and art. I rented an apartment on barter and moved both my business and my household furnishings. I eat at barter restaurants and stay at barter hotels. There are dentists, accountants, chiropractors, and morticians in the exchange."

If you have a small-business practice and time on your hands, joining a barter exchange may open a new market to you.

51. Strike up a conversation with the business traveler next to you on your next plane trip. Corporate financial guidelines require nearly everyone to ride in coach these days. You can network with bank presidents, environmental consultants, and corporate bigwigs of every stripe at 50,000 feet.

"I always pay to fly first class—out of firm funds, not the client's. This allows me to meet key people in a natural setting where they have plenty of time to get to know me."

Chapter 4

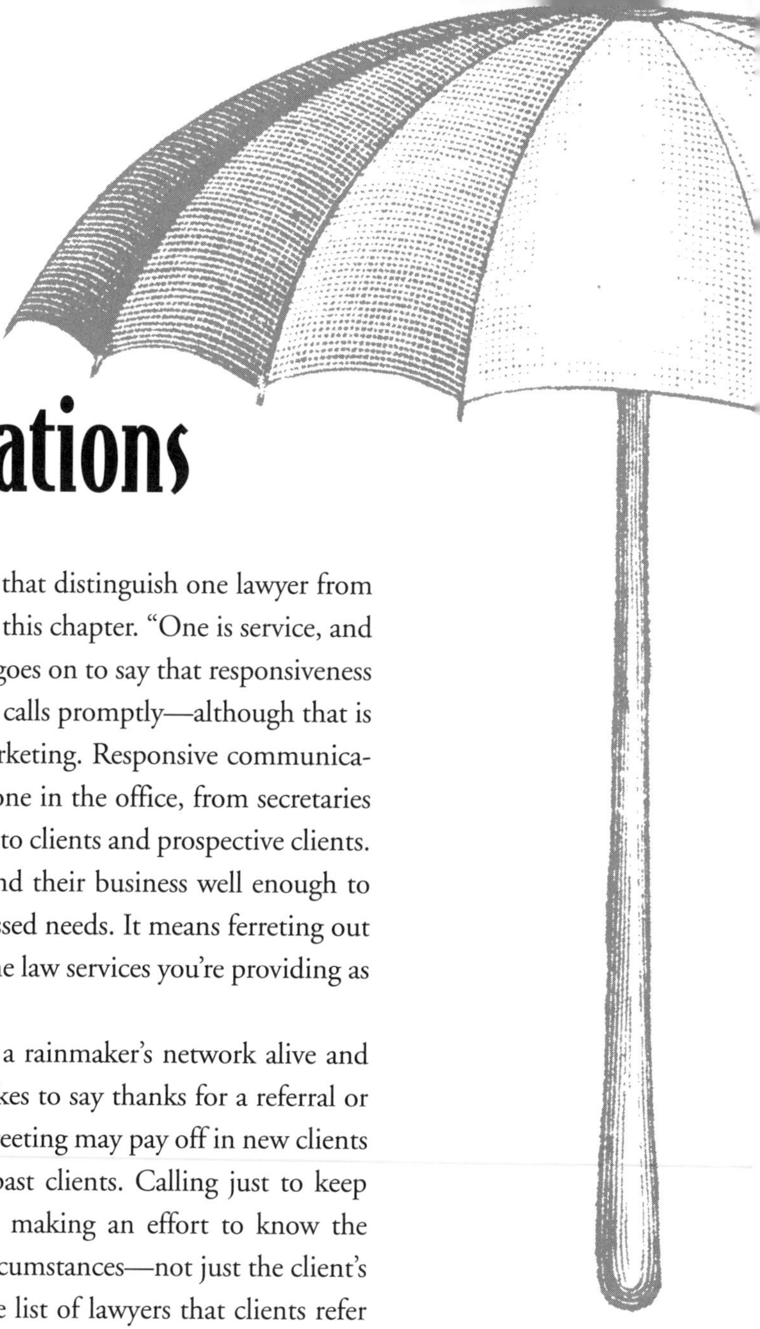

Communications

"There are only a few things that distinguish one lawyer from another," says one rainmaker in this chapter. "One is service, and another is responsiveness." She goes on to say that responsiveness means more than just returning calls promptly—although that is certainly crucial to effective marketing. Responsive communication means ensuring that everyone in the office, from secretaries to partners, listens empathically to clients and prospective clients. It means knowing the clients and their business well enough to address implicit as well as expressed needs. It means ferreting out what clients do not like about the law services you're providing as well as what they do like.

Good communications keep a rainmaker's network alive and productive. The effort that it takes to say thanks for a referral or to send a personalized holiday greeting may pay off in new clients or renewed relationships with past clients. Calling just to keep current on a client's needs and making an effort to know the client's business and personal circumstances—not just the client's case—puts you at the top of the list of lawyers that clients refer to their own contacts.

When you have reason to believe your client is not happy with your or your firm's performance, be concerned.

Ask if there is a problem and offer to fix it.

52. Developing effective and empathic listening skills is extremely critical for many reasons. To build effective friendships or effective networks, you must get to know other people, to know what they like and don't like. Learn about their hobbies and their family situations. Let them know you care about what's going on with them. Maintaining effective client relations means knowing when the client is happy and knowing when the client is not happy.

It's important to listen to and elicit client complaints. Client complaints really aren't bad news. Not hearing client complaints is really bad news. Learn how to check in with clients from time to time just to see—particularly if you've delegated work—how it's going. If you discover something is not going right, being able to respond is a very, very important part of maintaining effective client relations.

53. To retain clients, do a client checkup. Check in with clients and ask them if they are satisfied with your services and what needs have not been met.

Try to do a postmortem at the end of a matter to get clients' feedback. It may tell why you are not getting more business from them if you are not. You may find out that someone who was working on it with them offended them in some way, and it may give you some way to correct a problem if there was a problem. They may be perfectly happy, and if they are, you want to know that. Try to find out what you did well, what you may have done not so well.

Here's the input of an in-house attorney:

"One of the things that causes lawyers to lose business and is a real gripe among in-house counsel is when lawyers send us bills that include an increase in the hourly rate without having called to discuss it first. I can assure you the next time I send a matter out, I will not send it to the lawyer who has raised rates without notice. There need not have been a lot of money at issue. The rate may not be any higher than that of another firm we use. But just raising the rates by $10 at the end of the year and sending a little notice with the bill that the rate is now $10 more is not a way to do business with me.

"The way to do business with me is to discuss your need for a rate increase. We need to sit down and try to work out whether or not we are willing to pay more. I am budgeted, and part of my incentive pay is based on my managing my legal fees. I can't afford to get into circumstances where you have now raised what the litigation costs are going to be. When I set up a budget with you, I expect you to stay within that budget and not to write me a letter to say we are going over budget and this is what is happening. Unfortunately, this happens all too frequently."

54. There are only a few things that distinguish one lawyer from another. One is service, and another one is responsiveness. You can be a great lawyer, but if you don't return your telephone calls you are not going to have the client. One lawyer attributes her success to always being very responsive to clients and interested in their own work; not just the particular case of the day, but the totality of their business. Clients want to feel you are there for them and you care about them. When you have created that feeling, you will continue to receive their business. When they know someone else who needs a lawyer, they will say "Boy, do I have a lawyer for you."

Nothing is more effective than returning those phone calls the same day. If you are there until 6:30 or 7:00 P.M., clients will say

People today in positions of power get a great deal of mail.

They appreciate communications that are going to take the stress out of life; that are more humanizing and individualized. Make your correspondence as reader-friendly as possible. Clients want results, but they want them in a pleasant context.

Use business social stationery for a more personal touch.

This is about five by eight inches and has just the firm name and address without all the lawyers' names. It looks great and personalizes the contact more than regular formal letterhead.

"I can't believe you are still at the office calling me." You may be calling them from home, but it doesn't make any difference. You still care enough to get back to them. That is one of the most impressive things you can do, particularly with new clients.

55. Staying in touch with people—sending thank you notes, birthday cards, and all types of personalized communication—is very important.

56. Keep a collection of greeting cards in the office. You can dash one off upon learning of a client's illness, marriage, job promotion, or a death in the family. Many companies now make cards specifically for use among business colleagues.

A very simple thing to do is send holiday cards to all past clients. One attorney reports this experience:

"I had a client come in that I had previously represented on a small employment matter. I hadn't seen him for a year or more. When he decided he wanted to get a divorce, he came in carrying the holiday card I had sent a few months earlier saying 'I'm glad I found this. My wife just left me and now I need a divorce.'"

Any kind of Season's Greetings cards with a little personal touch (make sure you sign it with your own handwriting) works. It does seem to impress people that you took the time to send them a card.

Don't send greeting cards only at holidays. There is a line of cards called Corporate Courtesies (800/779–2779) that is a woman-owned company. They are very dignified navy, white, or burgundy cards, and women rainmakers report very nice feedback. A commonly used card says "Thank you for your referral." There is another one, "Enjoyed meeting with you."

57. Remember what your mother taught you: write thank you letters for *everything.* (Or make thank you calls immediately following the meeting or other occasion.)

"Whenever I get a referral from someone, I always write a letter saying thank you for the referral, but I also note the referral in my file. When the matter is completed, I write to the person that referred it and say thanks again and indicate what happened so he or she knows what the outcome of that case was. This often leads to another referral."

"Don't underestimate a plain thank you note. I had a form thank you letter on the computer, but it still wasn't getting out in a timely fashion. There was always something more important that the staff had to get out. I find handwritten notes are getting much better feedback because people know that they are not some form letter on the computer.'

58. It's amazing how much people do appreciate beautiful, thoughtfully chosen holiday cards. Even if the firm has a master list, keep a personal list for sending in your own name. *Sign* your name on the card. Holiday cards are a traditional, ethical way to show clients and potential clients you are thinking about them.

Worse than not sending any cards at all is to send cards that simply have your name imprinted on them. One lawyer reports she was taught this lesson rather severely the first year that she sent out imprinted cards without a personal signature. A furious client

Encourage clients to let you know what they like—and what they would like different.

Learn the names of your client's family members.

You can inquire about them by name and say hello if you have to call the home.

called to say "If you don't have the time and I'm not important enough to personalize the cards, don't waste everybody's time and money by doing this!" Obviously the lawyer was not pleased with this reaction, but it made her stop and think. She decided the client was right and now takes the time to sign all her cards.

Not only should you personally sign every one of your holiday greeting cards, but always try to write some kind of personal note. Of course it is important to know your client's business, but it is also important for clients to feel you are interested in them as people and know them individually and know what they are interested in so that you can personalize your relationship.

59. Respond *immediately* to client requests. Responsiveness is the single most important reason clients give for giving a lawyer repeat business.

If you can't return a phone call, have your secretary call and say you're unavailable right now, but ask if anyone else can help or ask the client to explain fully what is needed and say that your secretary will convey the information when you call in.

60. Do all you can to make the client feel he or she is the most important client you have.

61. Learn the names of your client's business partners and associates, even if you are representing the client on a personal matter. Make the receptionist, administrative assistant, and secretary your friends.

Really get to know your clients' business or occupation, even if you are representing them in an unrelated matter. Refer business to your clients whenever possible. They then benefit from knowing you separately from your legal work. Even with people who are not currently your clients, try to refer business to others. These people then know you are concerned about their business and therefore will consider you in a positive light when their need for a lawyer arises.

Give clients your home number.

For better or worse, when there's an emergency, you'll be the one to get the call.

62. Many new clients will simply go on to the next lawyer on their list if they can't reach you. If you're unavailable, you may want to have your secretary give the caller an appointment.

Order conferencing and call forwarding features for your home phone. Keep your answering machine on whenever you are unavailable to take calls.

63. Have a direct-dial line. Answer your own phone whenever possible.

Pick up your voice mail as frequently as you pick up messages from your secretary or receptionist. Return calls at least twice a day. Your secretary should always know where you can be reached.

64. Visit the client's place of business and meet the middle managers as well as the officers. Ask for a tour and meet the people who produce the client's product or perform the services.

Read the trade papers relevant to your clients' industries.

65. Call your clients regularly for no reason at all. Clients appreciate a "no charge" phone call from

Voice mail can be a big turnoff.

Change your message frequently. Make sure the message provides instructions to allow talking to a human. Be sure that the human will take a message, not refer the caller back to voice mail.

their lawyer who just wants to check in and say "Hi. How are you doing?" They may be shocked at first. If you get your clients talking about what's new in their lives, you may uncover a need for legal services of which the client was unaware. Don't think of this as a sales call, though, so much as a social one: no hard sell! Keep checking in through months of no activity. When that client does need legal services, you'll be there to help.

66. Make sure callers are greeted politely and promptly. Your receptionist is a caller's first impression of the firm. This one area has generated more complaints than you can imagine. Ask a friend to call your office while you listen on an extension or speakerphone. How is that person greeted? Are there long periods on hold? Are messages taken thoroughly, promptly, and courteously?

If someone calls for information on your firm, is the receptionist supposed to respond or refer the matter? Many receptionists have turned away business because either they were unaware of the breadth of the firm's practice or (obviously) they were untrained in spotting the correct legal issue when callers explained their business. You will have to weigh the loss of your time if you personally field these calls versus the loss of good business your receptionist may be turning away. If you do take the call and then don't accept the case, you should probably follow up with a letter memorializing that you did not accept professional responsibility to avoid a potential malpractice action later.

Marketing goes all the way through your staff. If clients adore your secretary, then you get more business. If you are out of the office, clients can still call for information, asking specifically for your assistant. Because they know her and trust her, they know she is going to get that message to you. The vast majority of clients realize that you can't always be available for their call.

When you hire a secretary, one of the first things to ask is "Tell me what your concept of marketing is." Everyone in your office, including that new secretary, paralegals, and file clerks, should receive marketing training. When clients know the whole staff and like all of them, they are comfortable when the attorney is not immediately at the helm.

Let clients know you saw their name (favorably) in the news.

67. One rainmaker's firm has a very effective in-house program to teach marketing. The modules covered issues like listening skills, initial client interviews, client complaints. Most of the communication techniques were oriented toward eliciting information from clients.

There was a module on cross-selling. Again, that employed listening communication skills to learn about marketing opportunities with existing clients.

There was a module on billing with a variety of approaches to establishing billing practices, retainers, and the sort of frank financial conversation that is sometimes difficult for people.

Too often, lawyers continue to submit bills on some form that was set up years ago. In this progressive firm's bills, lawyers try to include an extensive narrative of the activity that was undertaken. To say simply "Will and trust: $X" doesn't tell very much. But a description such as "Analysis of family and financial facts, in-depth consultation with client" shows the client what was involved. Another lawyer in this firm always includes a cover letter commenting on the case, thereby personalizing the bill, an excellent marketing technique.

Bills that include narrative reminding the client what this lawyer has done for the last month or three months or six

Send copies of articles of interest with a short note and your business card.

months make a lot more sense and generate a lot more goodwill than the ones without any kind of description.

Billing can be an effective marketing tool. The trend in the marketplace now favors

- bills that provide clear trails of what the lawyers have been doing and
- arrangements other than hourly billing—for instance, unit billing—as alternatives to try to control costs.

68. Send information culled from law reporters in your field to your clients.

69. "When you have a firm with offices in different states, it is very important to let your clients know you practice in multiple jurisdictions. Many of my clients didn't know we had a practice in New Jersey when they had problems in New Jersey. When I let them know I was the managing partner of our New Jersey office, they were surprised. So let your clients know. They don't always look at the letterhead that lists both offices."

70. "Negative comments about other lawyers are really counterproductive. That sort of thing never works. It does pay to promote other people. It pays to promote other lawyers. It pays to promote other lawyers in your firm. It pays to promote other lawyers on the other side of deals or transactions; it never pays to put down competition.

"I was at a meeting with a lawyer who sought to impress the client with derogatory remarks about the quality of the representation of the party on the other side. The client never said anything in the course of that conversation, just nodded. Afterward she remarked that she was so offended by that kind of negative commentary that she never wanted to do business with the fellow I had come in with again."

71. Be an information broker. Get on newsletter mailing lists from accounting firms, other lawyers, the U.S. Small Business Association, national industry-specific organizations, and local business groups. One of the benefits of joining organizations and attending functions is that you may receive a free subscription to a valuable publication.

A brief perusal of this volume of mail will empower you to speak intelligently on a wide range of topics that may impact your clients. You may not know all the answers, but at least you will have a pretty good idea of the questions.

72. Make "house calls." Hardly any lawyers extend to their clients the courtesy of going to their client's office rather than having the client come to their office, but it pays off.

"When I get back a nice set of interrogatory answers from some middle manager who stayed up late or worked a weekend to get these responses to me, I write that manager a personal thank you, and I let the supervisor know what a good job he or she did for me. I found this gives me a lot of goodwill in the companies and gives me more business."

Read *The Wall Street Journal* every day.

You can always find an article of interest to one of your clients to send on. Read every business publication you can. Forbes, Business Week, *and especially local business publications are all good information sources.*

Chapter 5

Public Relations

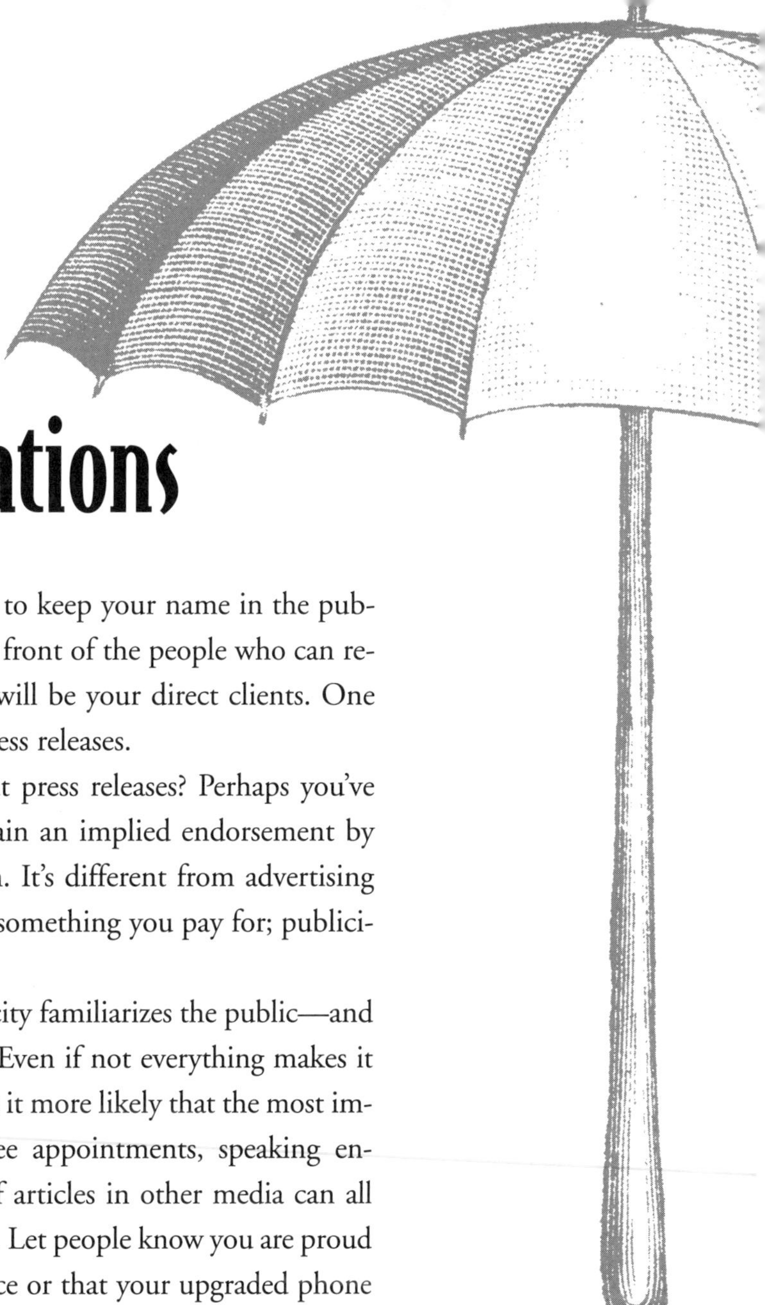

As a rainmaker, you want to keep your name in the public eye. You want to keep it in front of the people who can refer business to you and who will be your direct clients. One way to do so is to send out press releases.

Why should you send out press releases? Perhaps you've heard that press releases contain an implied endorsement by the medium that carries them. It's different from advertising in that respect. Advertising is something you pay for; publicity is something you beg for.

A stream of positive publicity familiarizes the public—and the media—with your name. Even if not everything makes it to print, that familiarity makes it more likely that the most important stories do. Committee appointments, speaking engagements, and publication of articles in other media can all be the subject of a press release. Let people know you are proud of the new lawyer in your office or that your upgraded phone system now provides direct-dial numbers for every lawyer. People remember the name of the lawyer they heard from last.

The more people see your name, the more they're likely to remember you when it comes time for representation.

73. Having your name appear repeatedly in the media can bring you respect. One rainmaker who successfully publicized one of her speaking engagements reports receiving the comment "I saw your name here doing this. I knew you were a lawyer, and I knew you did civil litigation, but I didn't realize you practiced in this area." Press releases have a cumulative effect. The more people see your name, the more they're likely to remember you when it comes time for representation, even if it's only to call you up and ask you for a referral to somebody else, a wonderful way to build business networks, by the way.

When you're talking about press releases, you're really talking about two things: you're talking about the release itself (or the piece) and you're talking about your media outlet list—who is going to get the press release.

Who should prepare the release? Some possibilities are your marketing person in the law firm and outside PR professionals, or you might do it yourself. Some lawyers believe it takes as much time to work with outside PR professionals as it does to do the job themselves. Also, PR professionals have been known to make some very famous mistakes. For more on this subject, look at the article in the April 1991 issue of *Practical Lawyer* magazine, "Working with a Public Relations Professional" by Theda Snyder and Tom Mulroy. The article discusses how to hire and work with a PR professional.

Who should be on your media outlet list? Certainly you're going to include the major dailies in your community, your business or industry publications, neighborhood papers, legal publications, and publications of organizations to which you belong. Personalize the piece for the recipient if at all possible. If it is going to your alumni news, include the year you graduated and the school or the college. If it's going to your neighborhood paper, make sure you indicate that you're a resident of that neigh-

Every rainmaker should have a publicity still.

borhood. In a big city there are lots of neighborhood papers. It's important to say "I'm a resident of Lincoln Park, and I want to put this in the Lincoln Park paper." Is it going to get picked up by some paper in another neighborhood across town? No, they won't have an interest.

When should you send a release (or, in other words, what is an appropriate subject for a release?)? The answer is "at the drop of a hat." Just keep sending them. Some things you can put in your press release include a big case, appointments and awards, boards on which you serve, changes in your law firm, your speaking engagements. Send out press releases before and after. Did you attend a continuing legal education seminar? Now you may say, "Wait a minute. Who is going to publish that I attended a CLE seminar?" For example, in one local Business and Professional Women's Club newsletter there is a "News About Members" section. If the editor can include that Virginia Smith visited her mother, certainly she can include a blurb that you attended a CLE seminar on the subject of toxic torts.

Photos

Every rainmaker should have a publicity still. When you submit it with your release, print your name on the back of the photo. Photos tend to come in categories: the lineup, the handoff, the handshake, the ribbon cut, etc. Editors really prefer interesting photos if at all possible. Important for women rainmakers is controlling the photo. It is important for men too, but particularly for women, you want to avoid the cleavage or gam shot. Even if the medium has its own photographer, try to persuade your contact to use the photo you know shows you to best advantage.

Headline

Inclusion of a headline is optional. You don't want to create a headline that turns off the editor before she skims the piece. If

Write in active, not passive, voice.

you do include a headline, make it clean and catchy to ensure your piece is considered and not tossed.

74. ***The Writing***

The text has to be well written. It has to look like news of interest to the readers of that medium. Write in active, not passive, voice. In the first paragraph, identify who, what, when, where, and why. Often that is the only paragraph that is going to be published. Include a quote for interest. Lead with the point you want to emphasize. A release can be written with several different leads, depending on the facet you want emphasized. For example, for a seminar the lead could be the sponsoring organization, the seminar topic, or a featured speaker (see examples, page 53).

Community colleges sponsor seminars where you can go to learn more about creating press releases even if you are not doing them yourself. If you have a marketing person in your law firm and you want to learn more about the marketing process, work actively with that person.

75. A good public relations program never stops. You must continually bombard the media with, it is hoped, newsworthy information. Repeated assaults will at least make the recipient familiar with your name, enhancing the chance for publication of any one article.

Because publicity is packaged as news, the information carries with it the implied endorsement of the medium. Board appointments, speaking engagements, and precedent-creating successes can all be subjects of press releases. Some publications, such as neighborhood papers and your alumni news, may reprint just about any press release. Others may be quite difficult to crack.

The Mechanics of Press Releases

Letterhead

Use letterhead for your press release. It lends credibility.

Contact

Show the contact name and direct-dial phone number.

Type

Press releases will not be accepted unless they are typed or word-processed using black ink. Avoid using script type and always double-space. Use upper- and lowercase type. Do not use all capital letters or underline words for emphasis.

One Side Only

Use only one side of 8½- by 11-inch white paper. Do not send carbon copies, onionskin, postcards, flyers, or odd-sized paper. Reproduced copies are acceptable if clear and legible.

Margins

Leave two-inch margins on both sides. Editors need room to edit.

Date

The date the article is available for publication or *FOR IMMEDIATE RELEASE* should appear as a headline or in the upper left corner of the page.

Identify

Be sure all titles and names are correct and spelled correctly. Always include full first name or two initials and a last name.

Deadlines

Make sure you know how far in advance you must send your release. *If you miss a deadline, you have missed your public.*

Quote

Use direct quotes whenever possible. A good quote can make a routine story unique.

(Continued from page 51)

Be Accurate

Be sure *all* your facts are absolutely true. Excessive use of adjectives, puffery, or exaggeration can lead to irreparable damage.

Grammar

Check your release for correct punctuation and spelling.

More

If a release has more than one page, type *-MORE-* at the bottom of each page and number each page of the release.

End

Type *END* or *###* or *-30-* to indicate that there are no more pages.

Photo

Submit only black-and-white glossy prints for publication. Use no more than four people per shot. Use action shots (don't line them up). Identify the persons from left to right.

Keep trying. By the time an editor has seen your name on the fourth or fifth release, he or she may be convinced you're someone special readers should know about.

76. Publicity is cumulative. Potential clients need to hear your name and receive your message multiple times before it registers.

77. What is the best way to reach your target market? Analyze your own strengths. Are you an effective public speaker? Do you enjoy writing? If you agree to produce a weekly

SAMPLE PRESS RELEASES

For national release:

-FOR IMMEDIATE RELEASE-

The Women Rainmakers Interest Group of the Section of Law Practice Management of the American Bar Association will sponsor a program on "Women Rainmakers' Marketing Tips" on Sunday, February 2, 1992, at 2:00 P.M. at the ABA Mid-year Meeting at Loew's Anatole Hotel, Dallas, Texas. Women Rainmakers will hold its semiannual business meeting at the hotel on January 31, 1992, at 6:00 P.M.

Featured speakers include Theda Snyder, a litigator from Chicago; Ann McNaughton Turner, an environmental attorney with Vinson & Elkins of Houston; and Edna Alvarez, a sole practitioner from Los Angeles concentrating in estate planning.

For further information, contact the ABA at 312/988–5706.

###

November 27, 1991

For regional release:

-FOR IMMEDIATE RELEASE-

Chicago attorney Theda C. Snyder will be a featured speaker at a program on "Women Rainmakers' Marketing Tips" on Sunday, February 2, 1992, at 2:00 P.M. at the American Bar Association Mid-Year Meeting at Loew's Anatole Hotel, Dallas, Texas. Women Rainmakers will hold its semiannual business meeting at the hotel on January 31, 1992, at 6:00 P.M. Ms. Snyder is cochair of Women Rainmakers, an Interest Group in the ABA Section of Law Practice Management.

For further information, contact the ABA at 312/988–5706.

###

November 27, 1991

Postevent alumni release:

-FOR IMMEDIATE RELEASE-

Chicago attorney Theda C. Snyder (Law '77) was the featured speaker at a program on "Women Rainmakers' Marketing Tips" at the recent American Bar Association Mid-Year Meeting in Dallas, Texas. Ms. Snyder is cochair of Women Rainmakers, an Interest Group in the ABA Section of Law Practice Management. She concentrates her practice in civil litigation.

###

March 5, 1992

FORM COMMITTEE APPOINTMENT RELEASE

Release: Immediate

Contact: Glenda Sharp
Phone: 312/988–5584

METROPOLIS ATTORNEY SALLY SMITH NAMED CHAIR
OF AMERICAN BAR ASSOCIATION FAMILY LAW COMMITTEE

[ABA NATIONAL CONVENTION CITY, STATE],[Last date of convention]—Sally Smith, a partner with the *Metropolis* law firm of *Smith and Jones,* today was named chairperson of the American Bar Association Section of Family Law *Finance Committee.*

Smith was appointed by incoming ABA Section of Family Law Chairman ____________________ of *[City, State]* at the conclusion of the 199___ ABA Annual Meeting in *[Convention City, State].* The ABA, with 340,000 members, is the largest voluntary professional organization in the world.

The ABA Section of Family Law studies and develops proposals on such well-known but rapidly changing subjects as divorce, custody, adoption, alimony, and child support and on emerging topics including surrogate motherhood, domestic violence, and cohabitation. The section develops model acts and guidelines on matrimonial law issues and publishes two quarterly periodicals; section members have testified before Congress on several family-related issues.

-more-

SALLY SMITH, Add One

Active in the organized bar, *Smith* sits on *the Board of Governors of the Big State Bar Association, is a past president of the Metropolis Bar, and chairs the finance committee of the Metropolis Women's Bar Association.*

Smith received a B.A. in *history* from the *Big State University in Collegetown* and earned a J.D. from *Top Tier Law School, where she was elected to its law review.*

# # #

column, but your inclination, ability, and time commitments prevent you from reliably meeting deadlines, you may have done yourself more harm than good. If time is your strength, seminars and speeches might be the best exposure of your practice.

If you want to start a business practice, see what businesses you have some connection to. Say you have some connection to jewelers: find out where their professional association is. Then get a list of the local jewelers, send out something offering to do a business audit of their firm to reveal any exposures they have, and you can start reaching out to them.

78. Get appropriate help. For example, are you interested primarily in creating a brochure? If so, you may need someone with great visual skills and a handsome portfolio of artwork. If you need to better define your niche in the market, research skills are important. If you don't want print or television ads, be wary of someone who stresses those skills in the interview. Ask about other similar work the PR professional has done. Review samples of other product to see if it suits your taste. Make sure that you're on the same wavelength. Using a PR professional doesn't eliminate your time commitment to getting the job done. Getting the job done is not cheap if you want it done right.

Investigate classes on do-it-yourself public relations. Try community colleges or women's organizations. Learn what makes a good press release. Start sending out regular releases. You can write them or hire a professional. Your newly acquired education will make you a more discerning purchaser of public relations services.

Keep an up-to-date list of media outlets,

including legal publications, alumni bulletins, neighborhood papers, and major dailies.

Send bulletins to clients about new developments.

You can buy special paper that has a colorful newsletter design ready to go through your copy machine. Lots of designs are available. The finished product looks very expensive.

79. If you have never done your own public relations and are not feeling particularly bold, hire a PR professional for a limited time and learn everything you can.

Contact the communications or journalism department of your local college or university to inquire about bringing a public relations intern on board for free or inexpensive assistance. Alternatively, get together with another business owner and jointly hire a new grad, each of you taking responsibility for half the employee's time and compensation.

80. "Always send a thank you letter or handwritten note to a lawyer who refers a client, enclosing several business cards and a firm brochure. Cost to marketing budget: a first-class postage stamp.

"An out-of-state lawyer recently referred a major PI case to me as the direct result of receiving our brochure, resulting in a six-figure fee."

A firm brochure may be your first contact with a potential client. The best brochure for small and medium organizations will be an 8½ x 11-inch trifold or 8½ x 14-inch fourfold piece. Using desktop publishing, you can create an attractive, expensive-looking piece that can be changed easily.

81. Get to know the reporters in your community.

Always respond promptly to calls from the media.

82. Rethink the public relations value of your cases and community activities. You may be more newsworthy than you realized.

Sensitize all your lawyers to the public relations value of their cases and community activities. Create a form for in-house use to report speeches, board appointments, and awards.

83. Have your firm cosponsor a major charity event. The cost is often surprisingly small. If high-worth individuals—or their businesses—are your target market, this is an excellent way to enter that market with a favorable glow about you.

84. Every rainmaker should have ample black-and-white glossies at her fingertips. Pose for a head shot today. A plain background is fine, though some lawyers like to be photographed in front of their law library. Believe it or not, some photographers who specialize in professional portraits have a "library" backdrop.

Use a pocket folder for client presentations. These can be custom-printed with your firm name. You can buy folders with die-cut pockets for insertion of business cards. Paper of different lengths can effectively create a headline look.

85. Consider hiring a public relations consultant to help you choose a target market, fashion a consistent image, and execute a marketing plan. Count on six to 12 months before seeing results.

Market yourself to organizations that might be interested in sponsoring a seminar on your area of expertise with you as the

Make friends with the reporter who covers the legal or professions beat.

Feed the reporter stories and information that he or she would not otherwise uncover or understand. Be that reporter's best resource.

Put on a series of seminars in your office.

Hire a PR professional to brainstorm with you on the title, write the press release, and create a media outlet list.

featured speaker. Working with an established organization avoids the expenses of a self-sponsored seminar and lends credibility. Don't expect an honorarium, but you can expect to attract new clients.

86. You can upload a press release to selected media throughout the country through Business Wire (East contact 212/575–8822, West contact 415/986–4422).

Electronic distribution is fast. You save the time and effort otherwise necessary to research and create an accurate distribution list, and you are not dependent on the mail. Electronic distribution is accurate. The destination list is current. Electronic distribution gives you a head start among all the other press releases that a recipient may receive. Using this medium communicates sophistication and urgency. Additionally, the recipient need only download your release into her own computer to create ready-to-go copy.

You will have several distribution lists to choose among. Cost depends on how many outlets you wish to reach.

87. Send a letter to the editor. A well-written letter can have surprising results. Other magazines often call to follow up. You can publicize your views and earn favorable personal publicity at the same time. This is one way to keep your name in the public eye in your community.

Chapter 6

Writing and Speaking

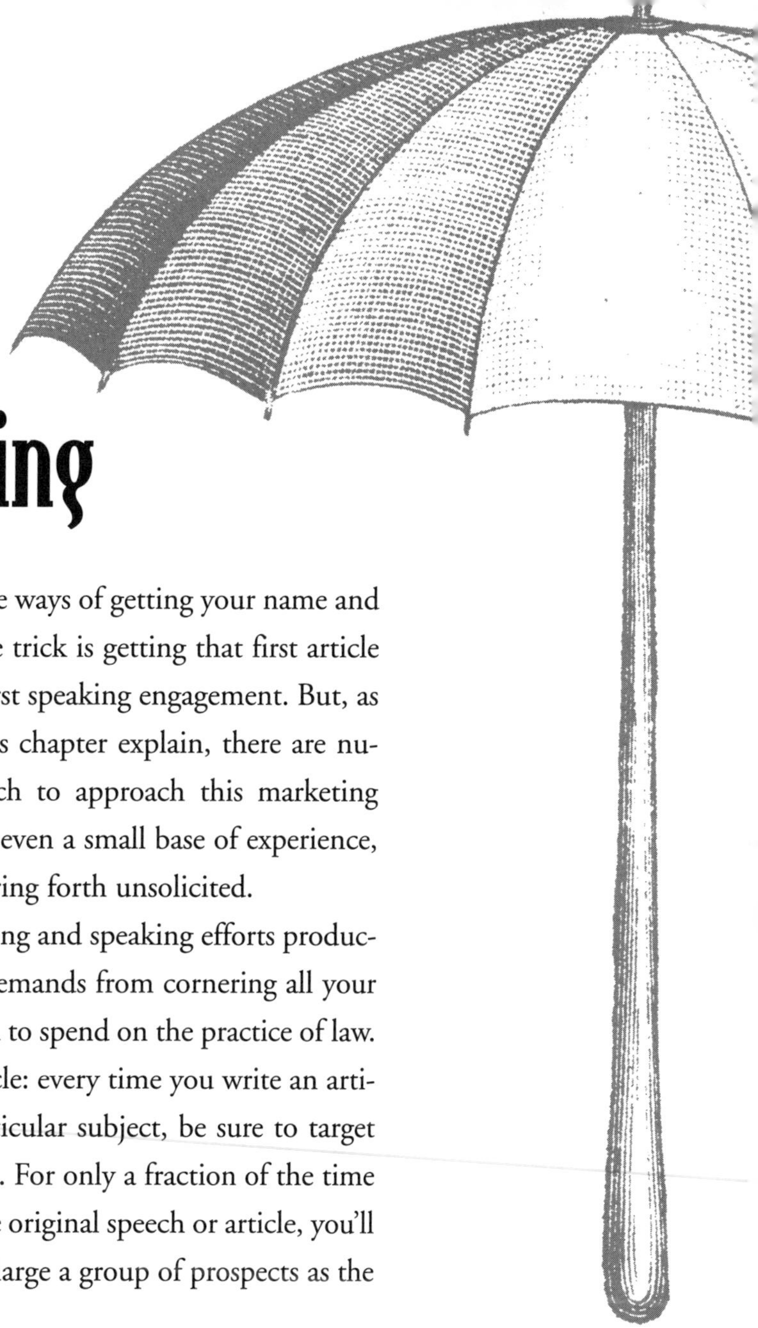

Publishing and speaking are ways of getting your name and your capabilities noticed. The trick is getting that first article published or lining up that first speaking engagement. But, as the first tip and others in this chapter explain, there are numerous directions from which to approach this marketing task. Once you've established even a small base of experience, new opportunities tend to spring forth unsolicited.

A key to keeping your writing and speaking efforts productive is to prevent these new demands from cornering all your time—time that you still need to spend on the practice of law. One way to do that is to recycle: every time you write an article or give a speech on a particular subject, be sure to target other markets for the material. For only a fraction of the time you spent putting together the original speech or article, you'll get exposure to potentially as large a group of prospects as the first time around.

Write on the area in which you want to make rain.

88. Every article on marketing counsels lawyers to write and speak to attain prominence. Yet nobody tells how to get the gig!

Continuing legal education organizations are inundated with volunteers' requests for a podium. Lay groups are difficult to identify and even harder to reach. What's the answer?

Speaking and writing bootstrap each other. The first slot is often the hardest to get.

Writing a scholarly article is probably the best way to start. Legal journals and magazines are always on the lookout for well-written articles. Write on the area in which you want to make rain.

Sometimes you can send a pitch or query letter to the publication asking if it is interested in a certain type of article. A negative response can save a lot of work. A positive response will generally provide length and style guidelines. Again, being able to write to the publisher's specifications the first time is the most efficient way to proceed. However, most publications will not commit without seeing the finished article.

Don't hesitate to publish in a newsletter or local bar publication, even if you really seek a wider audience. Many national publications, such as ABA magazines, regularly review local bar publications and solicit revision for a national audience.

You can recycle the same article with minor changes for different publications. This gives you maximum exposure for the same work. Naturally you want to reach totally distinct audiences. You may be able to rework course materials written to accompany a lecture for a law review article and then revise again for a lay audience industry publication.

Be alert to specialty publications for your target market. Virtually every category of professionals is served by a specialty periodical. The problem is all the lawyers who are already pitching articles to it. To stand out from the crowd, try writing on a new angle.

Keep your eyes open for newcomers to the periodical market. Read industry "what's happening" columns, which might announce a new publication. When you see that announcement, act fast. Write a sample article and pitch it to the publisher. Right now he or she is probably more worried about advertisers than writers. Providing typeset-ready copy is a blessing to the harried publisher. On the other hand, if you "write like a lawyer"—i.e., in redundant, lengthy sentences—forget getting published at all. No publisher will commit editing time to shape your article so you can get the PR benefit.

Keep writing. As new developments occur in your area, write an article. If you look over the periodicals you receive, you will see many articles are descriptive rather than analytical. Once you get the hang of it, descriptive articles that alert readers to a new development are really rather easy to churn out. Be first.

Once you are known as an expert on a subject from your writings, you are likely to get invited to speak. Knowing when to turn down a speaking offer is difficult. You want to reach your target audience. Yet, especially in the beginning of your marketing program, any exposure is helpful. Practice never hurts either.

At some point you will find you are speaking so often that you lack adequate time for lawyering. Measure the rainmaking effectiveness of your speaking engagements and adjust as necessary.

Always bring your own short introduction, which can be read verbatim.

Always bring your own short introduction, which can be read verbatim. Otherwise you may find you have lost some of the public relations value of giving the speech. The introduction should tell the audience about how you help people with problems just like theirs (presumably the issue you are about to

Offer to send a special handout to audience members who leave their name and address.

You can then use these cards for follow-up networking. This technique connects the person a little bit more to the firm.

discuss). This is the time to lavish praise on yourself since it will look as if it is coming from the moderator. However, a humorous, modest acknowledgment can break the ice with your audience:

- "Thanks, Henry. You read that just the way I wrote it."
- "Thanks, Henry. Of all the introductions I've ever had, yours was the most recent."

A light tone is fine, but, unless you are very adept at humor, avoid telling jokes as part of a professional presentation. When stony silence results, there is no graceful exit.

89. "I started marketing by teaching at a local law school. It had an extension program, and I gave an estate planning course for six women from Pasadena. Three of them became clients, and one of them is still a major client. I would speak for YMCAs. I would speak for any group that wanted something in my field.

"I don't do that anymore, because it doesn't sufficiently cull out the clients that I'm trying to attract from those that I cannot serve well. But early in my career I was starting from nothing, and I was trying to build a client base. It worked."

"I like to teach, so it's natural that I have served on the advisory boards of the USC Probate and Trust Conference and on the UCLA Probate Institute. By sitting on those advisory boards I'm making myself known to the other lawyers on the board, many of whom are from larger firms, and large firms have conflicts and need you at times. Because I'm a solo, I'm not perceived as a problem for the referring sources. I am not going to take other business from them. They know that they can refer this business to me and I will not take other matters.

"If you like to teach, get on the advisory boards of educational organizations for your specialty. You will get to know the other lawyers on the board well, many of whom may be from large firms. Large firms have conflicts, and from time to time they have to make a referral. Particularly if you are a solo practitioner highly skilled in a specific area, you may be perceived as the best recipient of those referrals. It is understood that you are not going to take other business from them."

90. When you give a speech, make sure your name, address, and phone number are displayed prominently on the materials.

91. Expand your networking list by lecturing to groups and offering to send an item of interest to those who leave their business cards.

92. The easiest way to get a speaking engagement with a nonlawyer organization is to call and find out who is the executive director. If you see in a community college brochure that somebody is teaching an adult education course in the area where you practice, you may want to call the person giving that course and offer to speak as a guest lecturer. Select these groups carefully to be sure the demographics conform to your intended market niche.

Virtually all professions have trade associations. The chamber of commerce or visitors' bureau probably has a list of the associations in your city. You must make a personal connection—call the executive director, take that person to lunch, let him or her get to know you. These organizations always want speakers. Provided this group is appropriate for your marketing effort, this is a sensible use of your time.

Women's organizations typically have a preference for women speakers.

Especially for a novice public speaker, women's groups offer a friendly, more accessible podium.

Offer to speak gratis in-house to select businesses.

93. Keep your curriculum vitae current. You never know when you will need to produce it in a hurry.

94. Never leave them without a handout with your name, address, and phone number on it.

95. Write your own speeches and publish. Take credit for what you've done.

96. "I would like to suggest giving a seminar for lawyers who practice outside your area of expertise about how two areas of law interrelate. I recently gave a seminar on the interplay of bankruptcy and family law. The domestic practitioners were unfamiliar and apparently uncomfortable with the issues. As a result I have received several referrals. Additionally, I now represent four of the attendees in disputes with their own clients."

Let your referral sources know when you're speaking or when an article you've written has come out.

97. Recycle your legal memoranda and briefs into publishable articles. Legal and nonlegal publications alike are always on the lookout for well-written articles. Don't stop at one publication. Rework an article for republication in various media aimed at different audiences.

See pages 65–66 for an example of an article placed in a national law publication, which was edited from an original article for a local lay audience.

98. Produce a newsletter in your specialty area for your clients.

PRACTICE POINTERS

Effective Drafting of Premarital Agreements

*by Theda C. Snyder**

Approximately 16 states have now enacted the Uniform Premarital Agreement Act. This statute codifies existing law and provides a framework for future legal decisions. Here are the issues the statute recognizes as appropriate for inclusion in a premarital agreement: respective rights and obligations in any asset; respective rights to transfer, manage and control such assets; disposition of the assets upon separation, divorce, death or any other event, or the nonoccurrence of an event; spousal support; wills, trusts or other documents to carry out the agreement; life insurance benefits; what state laws shall govern; any other provision which is not illegal. The agreement takes effect upon the marriage.

Sunset provision. Because circumstances do change, it makes sense to provide a *sunset provision* to terminate the agreement if the marriage lasts longer than a specified number of years, or perhaps if a child is born. Of course, the right of children to receive support cannot be contracted away.

Unless the agreement by its terms ends sooner, it lasts the length of the marriage. A premarital agreement can be amended or revoked at any time, but only by another written agreement signed by both parties. No money need change hands to make the amendment or revocation enforceable. If years later the spouses agree not to enforce the premarital agreement, they should formally revoke it. They should not rely on each other's word and mutual affection—too many things could go wrong. For example, after death, an independent executor would be bound by law to enforce an agreement which had never been officially revoked.

A premarital agreement will not be enforced if it was not entered voluntarily or the person seeking to avoid the contract did not receive fair and reasonable disclosure of the assets and debts of the other and did not waive in writing the right to such disclosure.

A premarital agreement will not be enforced if it is "unconscionable." Specifically regarding maintenance (alimony), if the terms of the agreement cause undue hardship in light of circumstances not reasonably foreseeable at the time the agreement was signed, a court can ignore the agreement and order appropriate support payments.

A premarital agreement makes a lot of sense in second marriages, where one party has children from the first marriage. Entering into an agreement can assure that assets go to a spouse's children from a first marriage, not the heirs of the second spouse. *(continued next page)*

Business purpose. A premarital agreement is a good idea for entrepreneurs, particularly when there are co-owners. A well-drafted agreement can assure all the business principals that a divorce will not result in an ex-spouse owning an interest in the company.

A premarital agreement does not bind third parties. To the extent either spouse contracts debts which could be construed as family expenses, both could be held liable, regardless of the terms of the agreement.

Some couples include provisions which govern their daily lives, such as who does the housework. The Uniform Premarital Agreement Act allows such provisions, but is most important in defining the spouses' rights to receive a fair share of property and support.

Usually, a premarital agreement is governed by the law of the state where it was made; but it can be governed by the law of any state to which there is a logical connection. This can be important if a move to or from a community property state is contemplated.

**The author practices law in Chicago.*

Reprinted from *Fair$hare,* January 1991, volume 11, number 1, with the permission of Prentice Hall Law & Business.

Volunteer to speak to school classes.

This is a good way to connect with the parents and the faculty. High school students may be in the market for a lawyer sooner than you might imagine.

A newsletter is a time-honored method for impressing clients and friends with your legal acumen.

Offer to write a client's business's newsletter or conduct a seminar for its customers.

99. If your local bar association does not have a speakers' bureau, volunteer to form one. You will be at the top of the list when inquirers request a speaker.

The most coveted speaking engagements are on radio and television shows. Consider putting together a promotional tape that shows what a fascinating speaker you are on some riveting topic.

100. Don't speak exclusively at CLE events. Rather, speak to the potential clients themselves. Reach them through targeted trade associations.

Chapter 7

Your Law Practice

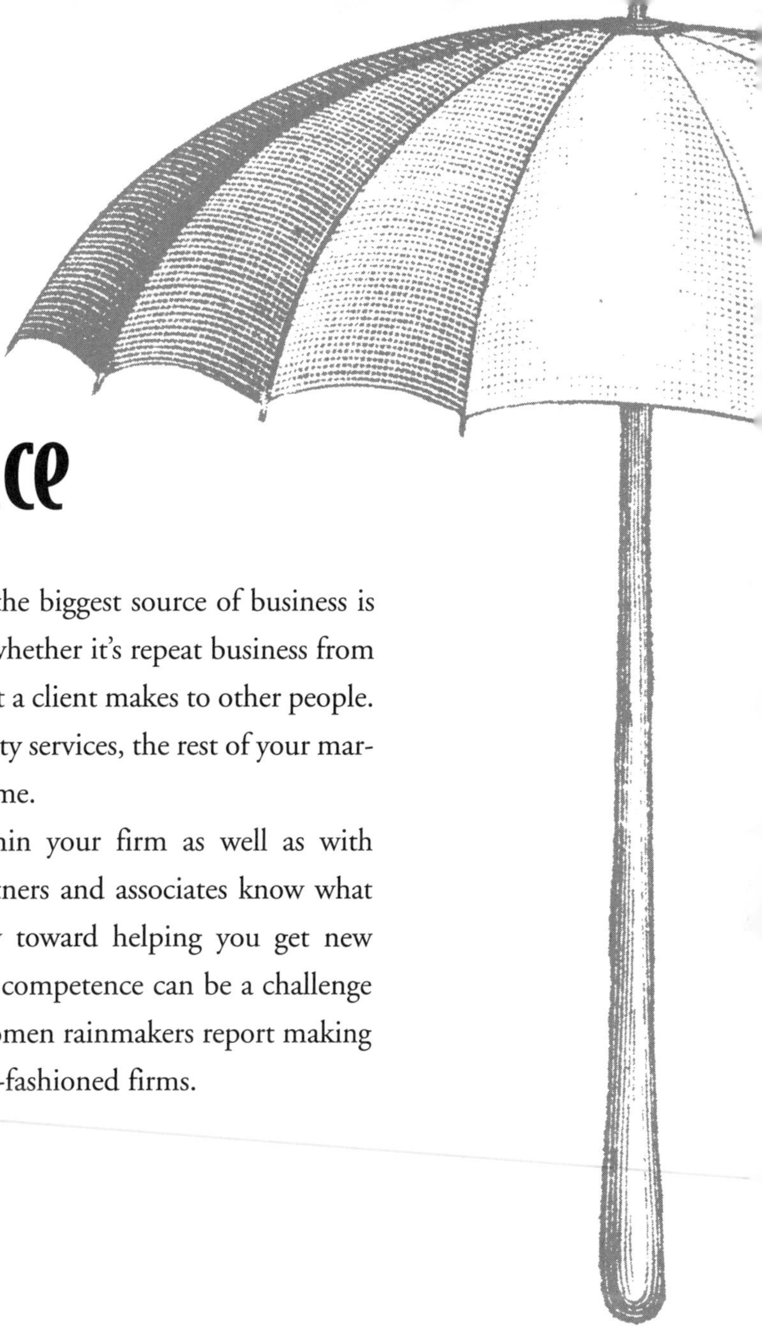

Every lawyer knows that the biggest source of business is from the present client base, whether it's repeat business from the same client or referrals that a client makes to other people. If you're not offering top-quality services, the rest of your marketing efforts are a waste of time.

This precept applies within your firm as well as with clients. Making sure that partners and associates know what you can do goes a long way toward helping you get new clients. Communicating your competence can be a challenge for women in many firms. Women rainmakers report making headway even in the most old-fashioned firms.

If your firm does not have an established pro bono program, get one off the ground.

If one is established, make sure you are involved in it. Pro bono work provides young attorneys with training and contacts.

101. Internal firm communications can be just as important to the rainmaker as communication with clients and potential clients.

For associates and young partners, you want other rainmakers within your firm to call you to work on their clients' matters. Building relationships with clients is the heart of rainmaking.

Partners should consider how clients are "bequeathed" in their firm. Retiring partners don't always pass clients down to the lawyer who did the most work. Do you project an image of capable management of client relations, besides your competence in your field? Work as hard on rainmaking internally as you do externally for maximum success.

Network within your own firm. Make sure the other lawyers in your firm are aware of your special skills. Cultivate lawyers within your own firm just as you would outside referral sources. Take the time to learn your colleagues' special skills to enhance your ability to cross-market the firm's capabilities.

102. The practice of law is your principal marketing tool once your practice gets going. If you're competent and caring or whatever adjectives your clients want—maybe they want macho and rough-edged—and that fits you and you perform well, and they know how you're performing well, you're doing good marketing. Those clients will refer other clients to you.

103. Any marketing effort must be founded on competent, top-quality legal services. None of this will be effective for you if what you're offering your clients isn't effective for them.

104. Take a leadership role in your firm. Within your practice area, volunteer to be in charge of marketing.

105. Make a file to give each new client that has the client's name and matter, your business and Rolodex card, and a pen with your firm name, address, and phone number.

106. Use the guilt factor. Partners want to include women and minorities. Confront or suggest to the managing partner that women be placed on all the most important committees, such as the points committee.

If your firm's clients resist having a woman assigned to the case, work through a front man, who will maintain the primary relationship but give you credit for doing the work. That person should try to gently educate the client.

107. Ask for marketing help and ideas from others in your firm.

Market as a team, not a solo. Going out on a marketing appointment alone sends a message that your firm is not behind you. This seems particularly true for women. Take at least one other lawyer along for presentations.

108. Open an account with a translation bureau. When a foreign-speaking client calls, you will be able to obtain an interpreter quickly with a minimum of fuss.

"Offer a free initial consultation.

This is often done through formal channels. I offer free initial consultations on international business transactions through the Federal Bar Association."

Deliver more than you promise.

109. "I garnered my largest piece of legal business by being courteous to opposing counsel on a legal matter. He remembered me and associated me on a large case when he needed help."

Chapter 8

Advertising

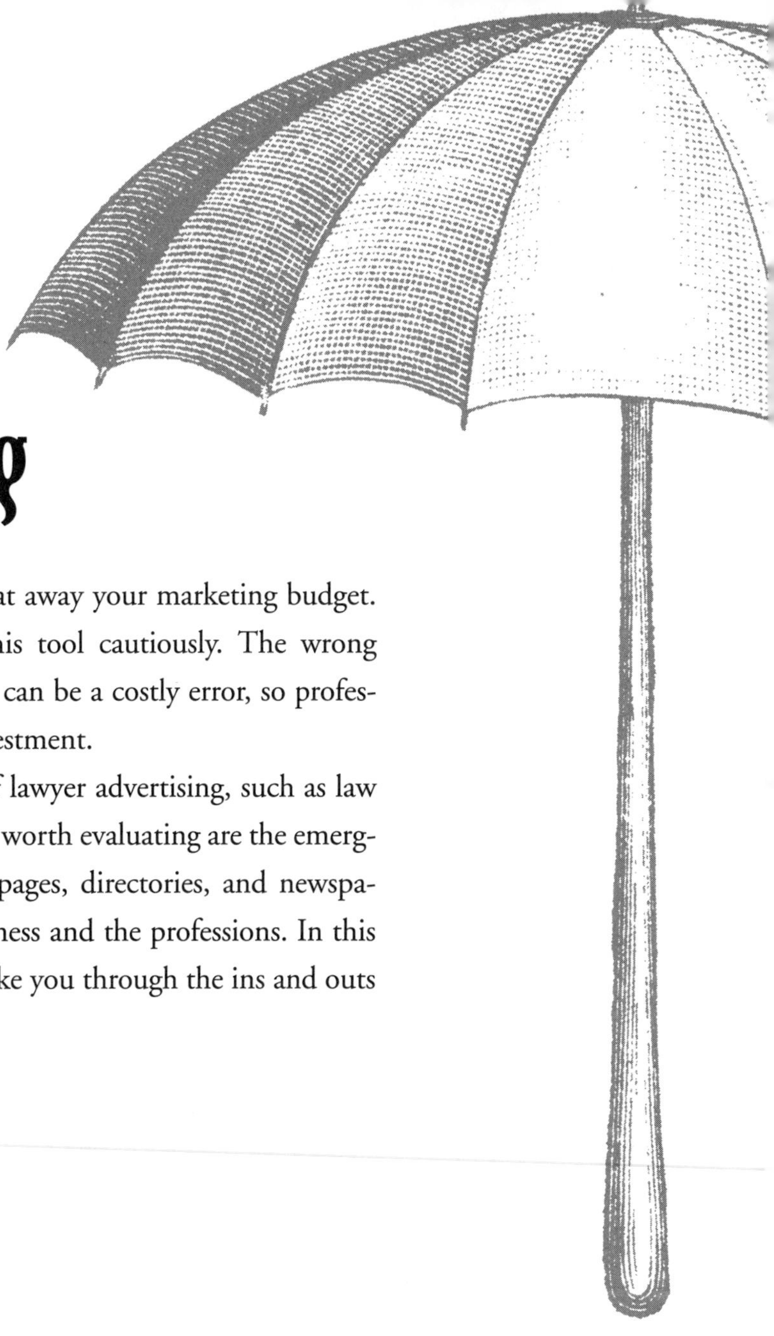

Advertising can quickly eat away your marketing budget. Therefore, rainmakers use this tool cautiously. The wrong message in the wrong market can be a costly error, so professional help can be a good investment.

Some traditional forms of lawyer advertising, such as law lists, often prove fruitful. Also worth evaluating are the emerging women's media—yellow pages, directories, and newspapers aimed at women in business and the professions. In this chapter women rainmakers take you through the ins and outs of all types of advertising.

Find out if there is a law list for your practice area.

110. There are lots of law lists. A law list—as opposed to a directory that might be put out by the state bar—is simply a list of attorneys who have paid to have their name in the book. Most lists are of attorneys who limit their practice to a specific area, although the King Kong of law lists is *Martindale-Hubbell* (800/526–4902), which is a general list. (Actually, *Martindale* is both a directory—the line listings in the front of the book—and a law list.) *Campbell's* list (407/644–8298) is also a general list. *Best's Directory of Recommended Insurance Attorneys* (908/439–2200, ext. 4462) is the bible of the insurance claims industry. Collection agencies farm out business through the eight or so commercial law lists. Three of the big ones are *American Lawyers Quarterly* (800/843–4000), *Forwarders List,* (800/638–9200) and *Columbia List* (800/645–8288.) Find out if there is a law list for your practice area.

Martindale-Hubbell Law Directory can be a powerful tool for attracting business particularly from lawyers in other states. *Martindale* is the only law list to rate its attorneys. There are three ratings: AV, BV, and CV.

To earn any rating, you must first qualify for the V, signifying "faithful adherence to professional standards of conduct and ethics of the legal profession, professional reliability and diligence, and standards relevant to the attorney's discharge of his or her professional responsibilities."

According to *Martindale-Hubbell*, the legal ability rating is based on "the standard of ability for the place or area where the lawyer practices. It takes into consideration experience, nature of practice and qualifications relevant to the profession. Where a lawyer's practice is limited or specialized, rating opinions are made on the bases of performance in those Fields of Law. There are no minimum periods of time in practice required for any rating."

A C means fair to high legal ability, B high to very high legal ability, and A very high to preeminent legal ability. That is why many law firms advertise that they are AV. A firm has the rating of its highest-rated partner.

Martindale sends out random lists of lawyers to rated lawyers. When the sales representative calls to obtain your signature for the renewal, he or she may also ask about lawyers who are trying to develop a rating for the next edition. Only an AV lawyer can say another lawyer is worthy of an AV rating. After you have been around a number of years, enough rated lawyers will recognize your name and think well of you for you to obtain a rating. Litigators get out and know more people. It's tougher for lawyers with an office practice.

After you have been around a number of years, *enough rated lawyers will recognize your name and think well of you for you to obtain a rating.*

You can shortcut this process by contacting *Martindale-Hubbell* and providing it with a list of lawyers and judges who know your work. This, obviously, is more productive than having your name sent to a bunch of people who have never heard of you.

Only lawyers who are rated at least BV can purchase a card (biographical description) in the book. Therefore, *Martindale* has a financial incentive to help you get at least a BV rating. Typically, you will have to spend some time as a BV before being elevated to AV status.

Supposedly, in some small towns the AV-ers won't accord anyone else an AV rating because they fear the competition. If you believe you are the victim of this practice, it is especially important to take the initiative in providing your own references. If you have an interstate practice, out-of-state lawyers may be the most generous in providing a reference, because they don't see you as a competitor.

Once you get in the book, experiment with your practice de-

Advertising will not work unless everyone in the office is aware of the ad and can respond to inquiries appropriately.

scription every year until you are happy with the flow of business generated.

111. Advertising can be effective when done well. Radio, television, or the daily newspaper might come to mind, but these are all very expensive. Don't overlook more targeted publications. Consider a church newsletter or local theater program for your message. Explore specialized ethnic and foreign language publications.

112. Peruse the lawyer advertising in the yellow pages for marketing ideas. You may be shocked. On the one hand, ads have gotten more sophisticated. On the other hand, some ads appear to violate the professional responsibility rules. Selectively adopt and adapt marketing styles.

There are a lot of advantages to using a marketing professional to create and place your ad. Not the least of these is an objective eye. This tombstone ad (a bare announcement of a transaction commonly used to offer initial public offerings of securities) appeared in the weekly business magazine of a major city:

Smith, Jones
Is Pleased to Announce
the Expansion of its Pacific Rim Practice
with the Appointment of
Los Angeles Partner
Teresa Manley
and the Opening of its
Hong Kong Office

While one might suspect that Smith, Jones is a law office, it might also be an accounting practice, an investment banking concern, or a marketing company. Nothing in this announcement says to the nonlawyer businessperson reading it what it is Smith, Jones proposes to do for its clients. It would not detract from the dignity of the tombstone one iota for Smith, Jones to describe itself as "Smith, Jones, Attorneys-at-Law" if indeed that's who they are. The folks at Smith, Jones probably figured they were so well known they didn't have to clue in anyone not in the know. The benefit of the ad is lost if it fails to communicate enough to attract the attention of the intended audience.

The benefit of the ad is lost if it fails to communicate enough information to attract the attention of the intended audience.

113. "Women's media" are becoming more common. Publications such as the women's yellow pages, published in a number of cities, are not aimed at reaching just women. Two are:

- Women in Business Yellow Pages
  7358 N. Lincoln Ave. #150
  Chicago, IL 60646
  708/679-7800
- Women's Referral Service & Yellow Pages
  13601 Ventura Blvd. #3221
  Sherman Oaks (Los Angeles), CA 91423
  818/995-6646

Check the bookstores. If you can't find the directory, call your mayor's office. Your nearest Small Business Administration office will probably have one—check with the person who handles certification of woman-owned businesses. If women small business owners are your market, this book will reach them. These books are distributed to corporate buyers who have a mission to assign business to women and minorities.

Women's newspapers serve an upscale—yuppie if you will—demographic group. *Today's Chicago Woman,* 233 E. Ontario,

#1300, Chicago, IL 60611, 312/951–7600 has published monthly editions since 1982. Similar publications are available in Cleveland, Columbus, Fairfield (Connecticut), Houston, and Phoenix.

114. Investigate collective television advertising. This can be very expensive with no guarantee of results. If you proceed, do so in a very focused way. Carefully choose your region and area of practice. One lawyer signed on to a service, choosing "wrongful terminations." He selected that area because the people who ran the service said there were many calls for that specialty and not very many people. He went in for three months, he maybe had eight calls and took four cases that turned out to be very solid and good cases, and he left the service.

115. One attorney put hundreds of thousands of dollars into advertising through Lutheran religious stations. Essentially, he provides information: his ads talk about why listeners need a will or the three things to know when you buy a piece of property or open an escrow or whatever. At the end of the spot, the announcer intones, "Brought to you by. . . ."

Over a period of years this lawyer has created a phenomenal niche. He now has five branch offices and a substantial practice. You can use that concept in your own areas of interest.

Chapter 9

Entertainment and Gifts

In the business arena as well as in a personal setting, entertaining and gift giving run the gamut from the conservative to the creative. As the suggestions in this chapter demonstrate, the possibilities are limited only by the individual tastes and preferences of the giver. Some women scrupulously avoid gestures that they feel stress their gender and undermine their professional status; others opt for what they're good at and comfortable with regardless of stereotypes; still others follow the traditional route.

Most women rainmakers agree that gifts and entertainment should fall in line with the image you want to project. So, as Chapter 2 advised, the key is to know yourself—and know what you want to be remembered for.

Insist that women be invited to all social/business-getting functions sponsored by your firm–even sports functions.

116. Entertaining a client can be as simple as going to a movie, a walk in the park or at the zoo or around the neighborhood.

A theater party seems to be a big hit with some people. If you're a theater buff, this type of entertaining represents the best possible situation; you are indulging in one of your personal pleasures, developing a friendship, and developing a client. Most business gifts and entertainment ideally follow this model.

117. In choosing how to entertain clients, pick things *you* like to do. There's no sense in pretending to like football if you don't know a blitz from a safety. Clients will pick up on your genuine enthusiasm or disinterest. It's OK to invite men to a ballet or opera.

Take clients to political and charitable events if you know the person well enough to know this will be an enjoyable—not stressful—outing.

118. Learn to play golf and how to bet! Consider a seminar for women lawyers on golf etiquette, betting, teams, and other kinds of sports.

119. Consider gifts that are somewhat personal. One Texas woman rainmaker reports: "A number of my clients are feminists. I give them copies of Mary Catherine Bateson's *Composing a Life* and more recently Clarissa Pinkola Estes's *Women Who Run with the Wolves* or John Gray's *Men Are from Mars, Women Are from Venus.*" Of course, choosing an appropriate gift depends on the recipient.

Houseplants or fancy food baskets at holiday time and for birthdays can be a big hit. Fancy fruits, gourmet meats, and every variety of delicacy wrapped in tinted plastic in an elaborate basket can be conveniently purchased by catalog.

If it suits your personality, give clients homemade cakes and goodies at holiday season and for birthdays, candy corn at Halloween.

120. The best gift is one that brings the giver to mind every time the recipient uses it. Therefore, the gift should be something that the client will value and use often, such as a credit card-size calculator with a likeness of your business card engraved on the back. Watches with a logo on the face—perhaps your firm's name—seem popular now. Advertising specialty companies offer a wide range of products for personalization.

121. "I never entertain clients in my home. I find myself acting too much like the little housewife, and that's not the image I want to project."

If you sense male clients are uncomfortable with you in a social setting, or if they treat a dinner invitation as a date, invite spouses/significant others to attend. Or try asking a male colleague to attend, or limit social interaction to lunches where business is discussed.

Some men will still not let a woman pick up a restaurant check. Make it clear when the reservation is made that Ms. So-and-So is the host and she is to get the check. Another way to handle this is to excuse yourself at some point during the meal and advise the maître d' that the check is to come to you. You can give the maître d' your credit card in advance, so when the check comes, it has already been put on your card. You need only check the bill for accuracy, add the gratuity, and put your card back in your wallet.

"I entertain people at home—either home cooking or take-out food. I don't usually use a caterer's services, but some people do."

122. A partner at an insurance defense firm sponsored a well-publicized alternate outing, a "Day at the Mall" for women adjusters. She arranged transportation to a discount mall and lunch. Supposedly there was a prize for the person who snagged the best bargains.

Chapter 10

Making the Pitch

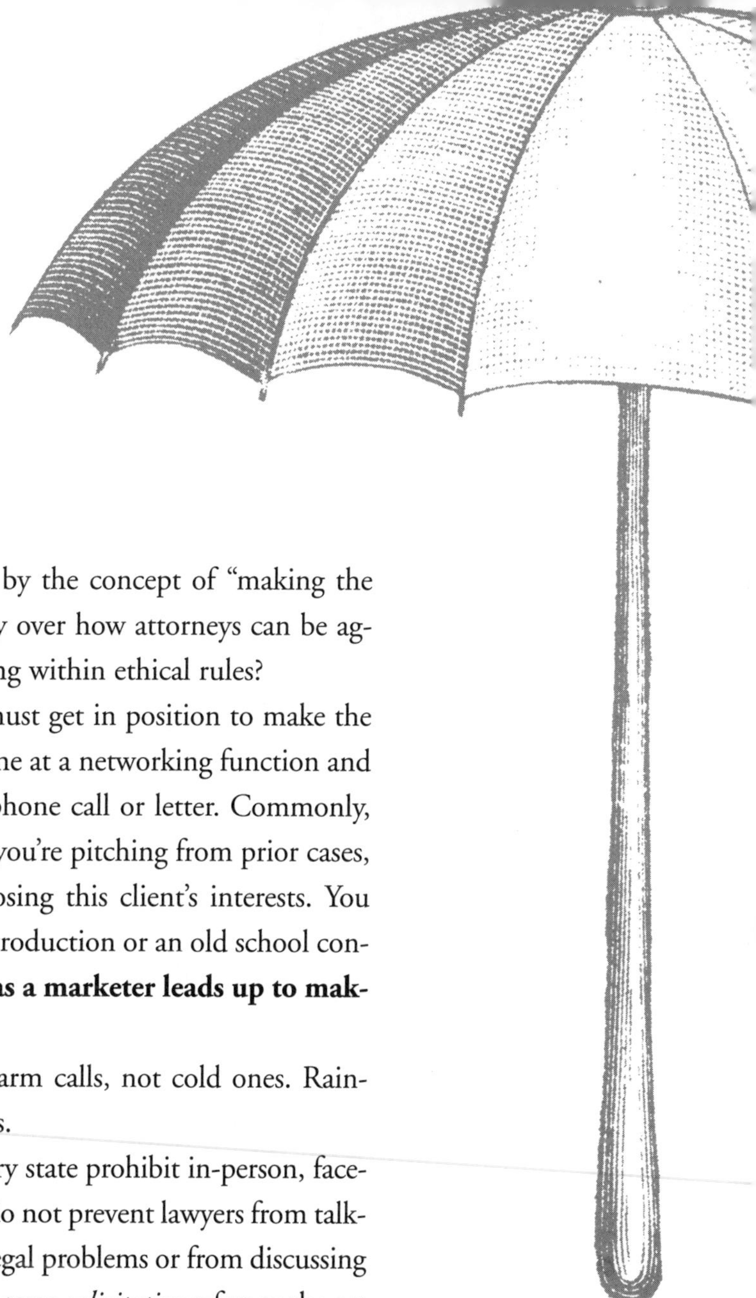

Are you totally confused by the concept of "making the pitch"? Are you in a quandary over how attorneys can be aggressive marketers while staying within ethical rules?

First, as a marketer you must get in position to make the pitch. You might meet someone at a networking function and arrange to follow up with a phone call or letter. Commonly, you already know the person you're pitching from prior cases, whether representing or opposing this client's interests. You may be following up on an introduction or an old school contact. **Everything else you do as a marketer leads up to making a pitch for business.**

Rainmakers only make warm calls, not cold ones. Rainmakers use soft-sell techniques.

Ethical rules in almost every state prohibit in-person, face-to-face solicitation. The rules do not prevent lawyers from talking to clients about potential legal problems or from discussing the lawyer's qualifications. The term *solicitation* refers to the act of suggesting the lawyer's availability to perform legal services

A rainmaker who skillfully develops a relationship with a prospect should never run afoul of the rules if she lets the prospect raise the issue of representation.

to someone with whom the lawyer has no prior professional relationship. Often solicitation complaints involve overreaching or hard-sell marketing techniques.

A rainmaker who skillfully develops a relationship with a prospect should never run afoul of the rules if she lets the prospect raise the issue of representation. If the prospect decides against the representation, the wise rainmaker does not press for reconsideration.

Smart marketers *do* initiate discussions with their existing clients. Strive to sustain client relationships by treating them as ongoing rather than one-shot transactions. The rules of professional conduct do not prohibit lawyers from seeking new business. For both existing and potential clients, you must ethically lay the groundwork for the pitch.

The best and often most aggressive rainmakers understand the limitations and never step across the ethical line. All the tips in this chapter (and throughout the book) assume that effective marketing is ethical marketing.

123. Be persistent. Churchill was once asked to speak, and the speech he gave was very, very short. He stood up and said, "Never, never, never, never give up."

Hungry isn't a bad way to sound, and aggressive isn't necessarily a bad way to sound. After you have done all the preliminary legwork and have created a relationship, the prospective client knows who you are and what you do. If you just say "Let me know if there is anything I can do for you," you have asked.

Sometimes it takes a little bit more than that. For example, you might say "Let me know if there is a new case that I can help you out on" or "if there is something to do on an old case that hasn't closed up the way you would like it to," or 'Don't forget that we are here to help you out anytime you need anything." Those comments are not terribly aggressive. They don't put people on the defensive or force a response. You don't want them to feel they have to explain anything, but you do want them to know you want their work.

It depends on whom you're talking to, but generally you can just ask. Say things like "I would really like to have your business" or "I would like to help you with new permit problems if you have any of those" or "If such-and-such is going to be an issue, let me know if I can be of any help."

To some people you might say "Why haven't you sent me any business lately?" People are not offended by that. They want to know who wants to do what kind of work.

One day I ran into a client and asked him why he didn't send me any more work.

He said, "You never ask."

124. Everyone involved in marketing legal services should adopt the notion that you need to let people know you want their business. You cannot assume that your friends will become your clients. It is your job to communicate to your friends and acquaintances what your business is and that you want their clientele. Be determined—but not invasive.

"Let the person know that you are interested in doing his or her work. I recently realized that although I had been working for a particular client for more than two years, he was not giving me any new cases. I was taking him to lunch and putting him in contact with other people who could help him in his work, but I saw no new work. Finally, one day I ran into him in the elevator and asked him why he didn't send me any more work. He said, 'You never ask.'"

Cross-sell the skills of others in your firm to the client who is reluctant to hire a woman.

Emphasize that the client will have available the full resources of your organization.

125. If you are in a firm with a number of practice areas, identifying opportunities to cross-sell is an important part of marketing. For example, if you are an environmental lawyer, you may be able to identify an opportunity for a colleague in the real estate section. The lawyer in that department can be expected to market back in turn. Marketing goes on both inside the firm and outside to the community at large. Effective listening is important to be able to identify those opportunities.

Never be afraid to suggest other areas where you can be helpful to an existing client. This opportunity often arises in the litigation context. While dealing with a specific litigation problem, you may find an area where the client is facing potential legal problems in the future—badly drafted contracts, employee policies, etc. Bring them to the client's attention, suggest a remedy, and offer your firm's services.

Sometimes it feels awkward to promote yourself with a client, but it is very easy to promote the other people in your firm. You can say "Jane Doe is our environmental expert, and I know you have some concerns in this area. Let me put Jane in touch with you, because she can help you." It is easy to promote other people; studies show that clients by and large do not know what other services your firm provides. They know what *you* do, because that is what you are currently working on, but they often don't know you have these other areas in your firm. Telling people about those other areas is cross-selling.

126. "I was representing a paper company, and, as it turned out, they were part of a big conglomerate, and actually the legal work was assigned out of New York.

But I had to ask at the local office where I was already representing them, 'How do I get more business?'"

127. When asking for new business, here's how to handle the issue of current representation and whether the prospect is happy with it. It depends on whom you are talking with and what kind of relationship you have already established with this person. But if this not a lawyer or you don't know the person particularly well, you do not want to merely say, "I want your business." Rather, conduct a more exploratory kind of conversation with questions like "What's going on?" and "What are you working on?" and "What are you doing?" If legal issues surface in this conversation, ask "What are you doing about those? Who is handling that for you? How is it going?"

You have a lot of learning to do about this potential client before you will be in a position even to know whether it is appropriate to market to this contact. If you conclude that the contact is a realistic prospect, decide how to raise the issue of representation subtly.

What if your request for business results in a response that another firm already handles the representation? Assuming that you know the firm, you might reply "Yes, that's a very good firm, but if they ever have a conflict, I hope you will keep me in mind."

128. To get business, you have to ask. Call existing clients and ask them what other matters they may have.

Your real goal is to reach that point in a relationship with a client where you can ask "What do I have to do to get more of your business?" Have the client then lay it out step by step. Once

Identify where business originates.

Staff at a branch or subsidiary company may be authorized to assign only smaller cases. Find out if you need an introduction to headquarters to receive the more complex assignments.

Asking for referrals is easier than asking for business.

It is never unethical to ask another lawyer for a referral.

you have that relationship—as you will—you can confidently ask for more business. The clients happily will give you bundles of information about their legal needs and what they liked and disliked about prior representation.

129. "I am in a small firm. Sometimes a person who can refer business may be dealing with a bigger firm, but there are matters the big firm can't handle. I met a financial planner, and she talked to me first about divorce business. She said, 'I send all of my divorce business to so-and-so,' and then she told me about this person's hourly rate, and it was astounding. I said, 'I don't charge nearly that much. He is a wonderful lawyer, and any clients you think are appropriate for him, by all means send them to him. But if you have clients who could afford more in line with what I charge, I would be very happy to have those clients.'

"I told her my associate does estate planning and we are very interested in estate planning work. She said, 'I send all my estate planning business to so-and-so.' She didn't tell me the hourly rate, but she told me who this person was, and I knew that lawyer was in a very large firm. I said, 'Surely there must be small estate planning matters that firm can't handle.' I told her that we are a very small firm and we are very efficient. We can profitably handle small estate planning matters and are very happy to have them. And now she sends them.

"There are ways to communicate your availability to people who think they already have lawyers, and someday I am going to steal some of that business from some of those big firm people."

Don't be afraid to tell anyone you would like more business: "I'd appreciate any work you're conflicted out of." "We're busy, but we always need new business—that's how we stay busy." Amazingly, many people assume a lawyer does not want new business.

130. Your best source of new clients is your old clients. Be sure to let clients know the full range of legal needs you can service. Ask clients to refer others who may need services similar to those you've provided to them. If a client compliments you on a job well done, respond by saying "If you know other people who could use our services, please give them my name."

"To remind people I want their business, I try to make it a practice with every bill I send out not only to write a little narrative but also to put a line at the end asking if there is anything else we can help them with. I have had a couple of people call me after they have gotten the bills and said something else has come up. The timing was such that it may or may not have had anything to do with our reminder that we are there to do more work, but it can't hurt."

131. Sell quality rather than price.

132. If you've been trying to get business from a possible source with no success, come out and ask why. Maybe there is nothing different you could do. Maybe the prospect won't tell you. But you might learn something important. Perhaps this prospect holds a misconception about your firm. Perhaps the objection is something easily changed. You aren't getting the business anyway, so there's no harm in asking.

Be enthusiastic about your special interest and practice area.

Tell people what you do best and why you do it better.

There are people out there who might not send you business because they think you are too busy.

133. "I purchased a car recently, and I asked who handled their legal work. I ended up representing that car dealership."

"I once took a general counsel to lunch to ask for business. We had previously been on opposite sides of a case, so we knew each other pretty well. Some men are uncomfortable with a woman picking up the check, and he tried to pay for the lunches. I told him, 'Oh, no, I am the one hustling you.'"

134. Sometimes looking successful can backfire. Several rainmakers report that friends or acquaintances say they didn't refer a potential client because they thought she was too busy or didn't need the business. If anyone asks if you're busy, respond "We're busy, but we can always use more work. That's how we stay busy."

If you have been working your marketing plan for a number of years, you may have achieved some degree of success and in fact may be perceived by the outside world as far more successful than you really are. What you may not realize is that you may be like the most popular girl in high school who doesn't have a date for the prom because all the boys think she already has a date. In other words, there are people out there who might not send you business because they think you are too busy.

"I have had the experience where lawyers have called me and said they knew I was busy because they see my name everywhere. This tells me my marketing plan is a success. Then these people ask if I could possibly talk to their next-door neighbor about a divorce. I am happy that happened, but I am wondering about

Ask for what you want.

the people who were put off by thinking I am not available. I think it is very important to communicate to people that you are available. One way to do that is by telling people, when they ask how it's going, 'Business is great, but I am always looking for new clients.'"

135. You've made the contact with a potential client. What do you do now to raise yourself from the level of "acceptable" to "most desirable" counsel?

Let's assume you've already learned the general nature of the company's legal service needs. It's time to get specific. What did the client like most and least about prior outside counsel? How are your own experience and expertise superior in substance and/or delivery? Be prepared to articulate why you are uniquely qualified to meet this potential client's needs.

State exactly the nature of work you are prepared to accept and what you do not handle (and why). Nothing impresses less than the appearance of wanting any kind of work at all. Selectivity confers credibility.

Be prepared to specify

- what cases you have handled that relate to the needs you would like to serve;
- what training, seminars or CLE programs, etc., you have experienced that uniquely qualify you;
- what technology, support staff, equipment, etc., you have to help you meet deadlines and achieve the quality you promise;
- what preparation you have undertaken for doing this work, such as research, reading, etc.; and
- what unique—even creative—ideas you have for this client's work.

Ask for business.

Schedule your meeting during regular business hours at the client's office. When scheduling your meeting, be specific about its purpose and length. An hour is more than enough, although 45 minutes is less intrusive and will demonstrate your superior organization! Enhance the probability of getting the appointment by suggesting alternate times from which the prospective client can choose.

In the meeting, get to the point early. Explain your analysis of what the client and the client's support team seem to need and want and identify what they've been getting and wish they had not. Explain your process and conclusions. Be very, very specific. Then seek feedback. Find out how they feel about your presentation. Ask for candor.

You're not finished until you have a commitment from the client to send you work. Failing a commitment, see if you can ascertain what else you need to do to earn work. If there is no match for you, determine what types of matters she does think you are well suited for and she is comfortable referring.

136. Don't be afraid to approach potential clients with preexisting legal relationships with competitors. Clients often need backup counsel when conflicts arise.

These recommendations assume your basic communication skills and sound judgment. A little common sense goes a long way toward making a successful pitch while avoiding ethical pitfalls. Good rainmakers can and do reach out for new business, but they always know how far they should stretch.

About the Editor

Theda Snyder is a lawyer in Encino, California. She has practiced in a variety of settings, including acting as principal of her own firm for ten years.

Ms. Snyder has published and spoken extensively on marketing topics for lawyers. Her articles have appeared in numerous publications, including *Law Practice Management* magazine, *The Compleat Lawyer,* and *National Trial Lawyer* magazine, and she has spoken before the ABA at Annual and Midyear meetings.

Ms. Snyder has served as co-chair of the Women Rainmakers and Law Firm Marketing Interest Groups of the Section of Law Practice Management. She is also a member of the National Association of Women Business Owners.

Selected Resources

Newsletters

Attorney's Marketing Report. Professional Publications Inc., 1201 Peachtree NE Suite 1150, Atlanta GA 30309–3522; 404/881–1141; fax: 404/881–0074; $197/year, $13/issue.

Marketing for Lawyers. Leder Publications Inc., 345 Park Avenue South New York NY 10010; 212/779–9200; fax 212/696–1848; $165/year, published monthly.

Practice Marketing International. Lafferty Publications, 2970 Clairmont Rd. NE #800, Atlanta GA 30329; 404/636–6610; fax: 404/636–6422; $520/year, published monthly.

Organizations/Affiliations

National Association of Women Business Owners. 1377 K Street NW, Suite 637, Washington DC 20005; 301/608–2590; fax: 301/608–2596; Publishes monthly newsletter *NAWBOtime.* Annual meeting.

National Law Firm Marketing Association (NALFMA), 60 Revere Drive, Suite 500, Northbrook IL 60062; 708/480–9641; fax: 708/482–9282. Publishes *Law Marketing Exchange Monthly,* a newsletter available to members only. Annual meeting.

Trial Lawyers Marketing, Inc., 1 Boston Place, Boston, MA 02108; 800/632–8400; fax: 617/742–5417. Marketing seminars for personal injury firms.

Women Rainmakers Interest Group, ABA Section of Law Practice Management, 750 N. Lake Shore Dr., Chicago IL 60611; 312/988-5619. Women and men dedicated to the education, marketing, and practice needs of women lawyers. Articles and column featured in the newsletter *Leadership & Management Directions.* Quarterly meetings. Membership includes annual *Referral Directory of Women Rainmakers.*

Books and Monographs

Grubner, Judith L., ed. ***The Last Frontier: Women Lawyers as Rainmakers.*** ABA Section of Law Practice Management, 750 N. Lake Shore Dr., Chicago IL 60611; 312/988-5522; fax: 312/988-5568; $9.95 (LPM Section members), $14.95 (nonmembers).

Itkin, Don. ***The ABCs of Marketing for Sole Practioners and Small Law Firms,*** 1993. Wisconsin Bar Association, P.O. Box 7158, Madison WI 53707; 608/257–3838; $25 plus shipping and handling.

Schmidt, Sally J. ***Marketing the Law Firm: Business Development Techniques.*** Law Journal Seminars-Press, 345 Park Avenue South, New York NY 10010; 800/888–8300. A looseleaf publication of approximately 450 pages, list price $95, updates approx. $42/year.

Videocassettes

Marketing Your Law Firm. Wisconsin Bar Association, P.O. 7158, Madison WI 53707; 608/257–3838; $149.00 plus shipping and handling. Shows how marketing principles can improve your firm's image and increase your business. Find out how trends in today's legal market should affect your firm's strategic planning.

Women Rainmakers: Strategies for Effective Networking. ABA Section of Law Practice Management, 750 N. Lake Shore Dr., Chicago IL 60611; 312/988-5522; fax: 312/988-5568; $19.95 (Women Rainmakers Interest Group members), $30 (nonmembers). Five successful women demonstrate how they make rain.

Articles on Rainmaking

Bean, Linda. "Women Who Make Rain Without Thunder." *New Jersey Law Journal,* Vol. 134 No. 15 p. 4 (August 9, 1993).

Carmody, Cris. "Women Rainmakers: What Starts as a Drizzle Can Become a Downpour." *Chicago Daily Law Bulletin,* Vol. 138 No. 113 p. 3 (June 9, 1992).

Eichbaum, June and Jonathan Lindsey. "Learning From the Success of Three Women Rainmakers: Women Who Develop Career Strategies and Offer Clients Added Value Are Succeeding." *American Lawyer,* Vol. 15 No. 9 40(1) (November, 1993).

Farr, Louise. "Bringing in the Rain: As the Practice Changes, So Does the Art of Getting Business." *California Lawyer,* Vol. 14 No. 3 70(4) (March, 1994) (Special Issue: *Women at Work*).

Killoughey, Donna M. "Ten Minutes a Day to Personal Marketing Success: Breaking Through the Glass Ceiling by Building Your Own Client Base." *Arizona Attorney,* Vol. 29 No. 5 39(3) (January 1993).

Morse, Nancy. "Rainmaking Key To Parity For Women In Law Firms (according to California Women Lawyers President Angela Bradstreet)." *Los Angeles Daily Journal,* Vol. 106 No. 9 p. B1 (January 14, 1993).

Rainmaking Issue, *Law Practice Management,* Vol. 20, No. 5 (July/August 1994).

Raridon, Susan and Eve Booth. "Rainmaker Role Is Fit for Women: Many Female Lawyers Hesitate to 'Market.'" *National Law Journal,* Vol. 16 No. 10 p. 23 (November 8, 1993).

White, Pamela J. "Rainmaking And Marketing; Opportunities For Women Attorneys." *Maryland Bar Journal,* Vol 25 No. 4 12 (July-August, 1992).

Zeldis, Nancy. "'Rainmaking' At Law Firms: The Last Hurdle for Women." *New York Law Journal,* Vol. 201 No. 82 p. 1 (May 1, 1989).

Zeldis, Nancy. "Women Lawyers Aim To Snag Female Business." *National Law Journal,* Vol. 16 No. 29 p. A10 (March 21, 1994).

Articles on Computer Software Useful in Law Firm Marketing

Cohen, Noel. "How Law Firms Are Using Database Information." *Leder's Legal Tech Newsletter,* November 1993, pp. 6–7. Leder Publications Inc., 345 Park Avenue South, New York NY 10010; 212/779–9200; fax: 212/696–1848.

Retterer, Jack. "Marketing Your Law Practice in the 1990s." *ComputerCounsel,* Vol 5 Issue 9 Sep. 1993. ComputerCounsel, Inc., 641 W. Lake St. Suite 403, Chicago IL 60661; 312/207–6900; fax: 312/207–1045.

Rumpf, Carolyn A. "The DOS and Don'ts of Marketing Data Bases." *Law Technology Product News: Products, Systems and Services for Law Firms,* March 1994, pp 30–31.

Seminar Providers

Marketing for Law Firms (an annual symposium), Law Journal Seminars-Press, 345 Park Avenue South, New York NY 10010; 800/888–8300, ext. 6111; fax: 212/696–1517. $495 price includes Schmidt, Sally J., *Marketing the Law Firm: Business Development Techniques* (see "Books").

Audiocassettes

Recording of *Marketing for Law Firms* (an annual symposium), Law Journal Seminars-Press, 345 Park Avenue South, New York NY 10010; 800/888–8300, ext. 6111; fax: 212/696–1517; $395 price includes Schmidt, Sally J., *Marketing the Law Firm: Business Development Techniques* (see"Books").

Selected Books From...
The Section of Law Practice Management

ABA Guide to International Business Negotiations. A guide to the general, legal, and cultural issues that arise during international negotiations. Details negotiation issues within 17 countries.

ACCESS 1994. An updated guidebook to technology resources. Includes practical hints, practical tips, commonly used terms, and resource information.

Anatomy of a Law Firm Merger. Provides information on every aspect of a merger and will help law firms of all sizes decide whether they should consider a merger.

Breaking Traditions. A guide to progressive, flexible, and sensible work alternatives for lawyers who want to balance the demand of the legal profession with other commitments. Model policy for childbirth and parenting leave is included.

Changing Jobs, 2nd Ed. A handbook designed to help lawyers make changes in their professional careers. Includes career planning advice from nearly 50 experts.

Flying Solo: A Survival Guide for the Solo Lawyer, 2nd Ed. An updated and expanded guide to the problems and issues unique to the solo practitioner.

From Yellow Pads to Computers, 2nd Ed. Thirty-five chapters with real-life computer applications that focus on practical solutions. Especially for the lawyer who's been too busy to use a computer.

How to Start and Build a Law Practice, 3rd Ed. Jay Foonberg's classic guide has been updated and expanded. Included are more than 10 new chapters on marketing, financing, automation, practicing from home, ethics and professional responsibility.

Last Frontier: Women Lawyers as Rainmakers. Explains why rainmaking is different for women than men and focuses on ways to improve these skills. Shares the experiences of four women who have successfully built their own practices.

Law Office Staff Manual, 2nd Ed. This updated version includes new sections on sexual harassment, alternative work schedules, and attorney publicity. Also includes the text of the manual on diskettes in WordPerfect and ASCII formats so that you can create a customized manual for your law firm.

Leveraging with Legal Assistants. Reviews the changes that have led to increased use of legal assistants and the need to enlarge their role further. Learn specific ways in which a legal assistant can handle a substantial portion of traditional lawyer work.

Making Partner: A Guide for Law Firm Associates. Written by a managing partner, this book offers guidelines and recommendations designed to help you increase your chances of making partner.

Planning the Small Law Office Library. A step-by-step guide to planning, building, and managing a small law office library. Includes case studies, floor plans, and questionnaires.

Practical Systems: Tips for Organizing Your Law Office. It will help you get control of your in-box by outlining systems for managing daily work.

Results-Oriented Financial Management: A Guide to Successful Law Firm Financial Performance. How to manage "the numbers," from setting rates and computing billable hours to calculating net income and preparing the budget. Over 30 charts and statements to help you prepare reports.

A Short Course in Personal Computers. Explains the basic components of IBM-compatible computers in terms that are easy to understand. This concise and accessible guide will help you make knowledgeable decisions in the law office.

Survival Skills for the Practicing Lawyer. Includes 29 articles from *Law Practice Management* magazine for the attorney with little or no management responsibilities.

The Time Trap. A classic book on time management published by the American Management Association. This guide focuses on "The Twenty Biggest Time Wasters" and how you can overcome them.

TQM in Action: *One Firm's Journey Toward Quality and Excellence.* A guide to implementing the principles of Total Quality Management in your law firm.

When a Professional Divorces. Discusses how to value a professional license and practice when a lawyer or other professional divorces.

Winning with Computers, Part 1. Addresses virtually every aspect of the use of computers in litigation. You'll get an overview of products available and tips on how to put them to good use. For the beginning and advanced computer user.

Winning with Computers, Part 2. Expands on the ways you can use computers to manage the routine and not-so-routine aspects of your trial practice. Learn how to apply general purpose software and even how to have fun with your computer.

Win-Win Billing Strategies. Represents the first comprehensive analysis of what constitutes "value," and how to bill for it. You'll learn how to initiate and implement different billing methods that make sense for you and your client.

WordPerfect® in One Hour for Lawyers. This is a crash course in the most popular word processing software package used by lawyers. In four easy lessons, you'll learn the basic steps for getting a simple job done.

WordPerfect® Shortcuts for Lawyers: Learning Merge and Macros in One Hour. A fast-track guide to two of WordPerfect's more advanced functions: merge and macros. Includes four lessons designed to take no more than 15 minutes each.

Your New Lawyer, 2nd Ed. A complete legal employer's guide to recruitment, development, and management of new lawyers. Updated to address the many changes in the practice of law since the 1983 edition.

Order form

Qty	Title	LPM Price	Regular Price	Total
______	ABA Guide to Int'l Business Negotiations (511-0331)	$74.95	$84.95	$______
______	ACCESS 1994 (511-0327)	29.95	34.95	$______
______	Anatomy of a Law Firm Merger (511-0310)	44.95	54.95	$______
______	Breaking Traditions (511-0320)	64.95	74.95	$______
______	Changing Jobs, 2nd Ed. (511-0334)	49.95	59.95	$______
______	Flying Solo, 2nd Ed. (511-0328)	59.95	69.95	$______
______	From Yellow Pads to Computers, 2nd Ed. (511-0289)	64.95	69.95	$______
______	How to Start & Build a Law Practice, 3rd Ed. (511-0293)	32.95	39.95	$______
______	Last Frontier (511-0314)	9.95	14.95	$______
______	Law Office Staff Manual (511-0307)	79.00	89.00	$______
______	Leveraging with Legal Assistants (511-0322)	59.95	69.95	$______
______	Making Partner (511-0303)	14.95	19.95	$______
______	Planning the Small Law Office Library (511-0325)	29.95	39.95	$______
______	Practical Systems (511-0296)	24.95	34.95	$______
______	Results-Oriented Financial Management (511-0319)	44.95	54.95	$______
______	A Short Course in Personal Computers (511-0302)	14.95	24.95	$______
______	Survival Skills for the Practicing Lawyer (511-0324)	39.95	49.95	$______
______	The Time Trap (511-0330)	14.95	14.95	$______
______	TQM in Action (511-0323)	59.95	69.95	$______
______	When a Professional Divorces (511-0326)	49.95	59.95	$______
______	Winning with Computers, Part 1 (511-0294)	89.95	99.95	$______
______	Winning with Computers, Part 2 (511-0315)	59.95	69.95	$______
______	Winning with Computers, Parts 1 & 2 (511-0316)	124.90	144.90	$______
______	Win-Win Billing Strategies (511-0304)	89.95	99.95	$______
______	WordPerfect® in One Hour for Lawyers (511-0308)	9.95	14.95	$______
______	WordPerfect® Shortcuts for Lawyers (511-0329)	14.95	19.95	$______
______	Your New Lawyer, 2nd Ed. (511-0312)	74.95	84.95	$______

*HANDLING
$2.00-$9.99....$2.00
10.00-24.99....$3.95
25.00-49.99....$4.95
50.00 +...........$5.95

**TAX
DC residents add 6%
IL residents add 8.75%
MD residents add 5%

SUBTOTAL: $______
*HANDLING: $______
**TAX: $______
TOTAL: $______

PAYMENT

☐ Check enclosed (Payable to the ABA) ☐ Bill Me

☐ Visa ☐ MasterCard Account Number: ______-______-______-______

Exp. Date: ______ Signature ______

Name ______ Firm ______

Address ______

City______State______ZIP ______ Phone number ______

MAIL TO: ABA, Publication Orders, P.O. Box 10892, Chicago, IL 60610-0892
PHONE: (312) 988-5522
Or FAX: (312) 988-5568

BOOK